THE DEVELOPMENT OF POTENTIAL COMMODITY BASED AGROTOURISM IN Around Mt. Wilis

THE DEVELOPMENT OF POTENTIAL COMMODITY BASED AGROTOURISM IN *Around Mt. Wilis*

Herrukmi Septa Rinawati
Tri Weda Raharjo
Trisnani
Abdul Hamid

www.whitefalconpublishing.com

The Development of Potential Commodity Based
Agrotourism in Around Mt. Wilis
Herrukmi Septa Rinawati, Tri Weda Raharjo, Trisnani, Abdul Hamid

www.whitefalconpublishing.com

All rights reserved
First Edition, 2022
© Herrukmi Septa Rinawati, Tri Weda Raharjo,
Trisnani, Abdul Hamid, 2022
Cover design by Bichiz DAZ, 2022

No part of this publication may be reproduced, or stored in a retrieval system, or transmitted in any form by means of electronic, mechanical, photocopying or otherwise, without prior written permission from the author.

The contents of this book have been certified and timestamped on the Gnosis blockchain as a permanent proof of existence. Scan the QR code or visit the URL given on the back cover to verify the blockchain certification for this book.

The views expressed in this work are solely those of the author and do not reflect the views of the publisher, and the publisher hereby disclaims any responsibility for them.

Requests for permission should be addressed to
septarinawati27@gmail.com

ISBN - 978-1-63640-776-0

PREFACE

Thanks to Allah SWT for His blessings so that the author can complete the book entitled **THE DEVELOPMENT OF POTENTIAL COMMODITY-BASED AGROTOURISM IN AROUND Mt. WILIS.**

This book is an implementation of agro-tourism marketing strategy involving village stakeholders and Tourism Office Regency which can be used as learning resource and basic learning for students. This book is expected to contribute on the development of science in academia therefore it becomes a significant book. to make it easier for readers to understand, author has arranged this book into several chapters.

The existence of this book expected to help students in expanding and deepening their knowledge to conduct studies in the required field of science. It is realized that during the preparation of this book, the author experienced many obstacles thus, it causes several shortcomings and still need improvement. However, thanks to the help, encouragement, and cooperation of various parties, this book was completed.

The author would like to thank family and friends who have supported and provided input in the preparation of this book. Therefore, the writer expects suggestions and criticisms that able to gain an improvement.

Author

TABLE OF CONTENT

PREFACE..v
TABLES..ix
FIGURES..xi

CHAPTER I: INTRODUCTION...1
             A. Background...1
             B. Agropolitan..5
             C. Tourism...13
             D. Agrotourism..14
             E. SWOT...23

CHAPTER II: ECONOMIC STUDY OF AGRO-
             TOURISM DEVELOPMENT BASED
             ON POTENTIAL COMMODITIES..........29
             A. Overview..29

CHAPTER III: POTENTIAL BUSINESS
             ACTIVITIES IN AGRO-TOURISM
             DEVELOPMENT...44
             A. Role/Support of Local Government......45
             B. Analysis of Internal Factors
                (Strengths and Weaknesses) and
                External Factors (Opportunities
                and Obstacles)...49

      C. The Selection of Strategy 73
      D. Potential Business Activities to Support Agrotourism Development..73
      E. The Role/Support of Local Government in the Development of Potential Comodity-Based Agrotourism 74
      F. Potential Commodity-Based Agrotourism Development Strategy...78

CHAPTER IV: CLOSING..83
      A. Conclusion...83
      B. Reccomendations..................................84

REFERENCES 85
AUTHOR BIOGRAPHY 88

TABLES

Tabel 1.1 Farm Area Typology 9
Tabel 1.2 SWOT matrix 24
Tabel 3.1 Weighting dan Ranking of Internal Variable Agrotourism Study 58
Tabel 3.2 Weighting dan Ranking of External Variable Agrotourism study 62
Tabel 3.3 Weighting dan Ranking of Internal Variable Agrotourism village 66
Tabel 3.4 Weighting dan Ranking of External Variable Agrotourism village 70

FIGURES

Figure 1.1 SWOT Diagram 25
Figure 1.2 Internal and External Matrix (IE) 27

CHAPTER I
INTRODUCTION

A. Background

Presidential Decree No. 80/2019 1c concerning on the economic development, stated that in order to increase the investment and regional economic growth which have an impact on the regional and national economy, the development of Selingkar Wilis and Southern Cross Areas is currently accelerated.

The results of the mapping of tourist objects indicated that the potential of tourist destinations in six districts is dominantly centered around the peak of Wilis circle and the potential tourist destinations dominated by ecotourism, Agrotourism, historical and cultural tourism, however it still not supported by adequate access yet.

As the center of agribusiness, East Java Province is focused on developing agricultural product centers and agricultural product processing industries in addition to market expansion, domestically and internationally. By placing Agribusiness as a system, it will change the proportion of Agribusiness's role in economy which has implications for the reallocation of more dominant economic resources to the development of Agribusiness.

Observing the development of agropolitan areas in Selingkar Wilis regencies with every potential they have, it is quite possible to develop agro-tourism and increase the additional value of agricultural products, for those that are in the potential, mainstay and leading commodities.

According to Tumenggung (1996:43) Leading sector is a sector that has comparative and competitive advantage than similar sector products from other regions and provides great value of benefits. The leading sector also provides additional value and large production, it has a large multiplier effect on other economies, and high demand for local and export markets (Mawardi, 1997:10). Leading sectors certainly have higher potential to grow faster than other sectors in the area, especially the supporting factors for several leading sectors, such as 8 capital accumulation, growth of absorbed workforce, and technological progress. The establishment of investment opportunities can also be done by empowering the potential of leading sector from the concerned region (Arifin & Rachbini, 2001:67).

Agrotourism defined as a series of tourism activities that utilizing the potential of agriculture as tourist attraction, both in form of natural panoramas of agricultural area and the diversity of production activities and agricultural technology also the culture of agricultural community (Palit, Talumingan, & Rumagit, 2017).

Meanwhile the definition of Agrotourism in Minister of Agriculture and Minister of Tourism Joint Decree, Post and Telecommunication Number 204/Kpts/HK/050/4/ 1989 and KM.47/PW.DOW/MPPT/89 concerning on the Coordination of Agrotourism Development as a form of tourism activity that utilizes agrobusiness as a tourism object which aims to expand knowledge, travel, recreation and business relations in agricultural sector. Agrobusiness defined as an agricultural business in a broad sense including dry land agriculture, rice fields, secondary crops, plantations, animal husbandry, forestry, yards, fields. (Mayasari & Ramdhan, 2013).

Scheyvens (2011) stated that trade in primary goods exports and tourism sector have made an increasingly important contribution to income generation and expansion of employment. while Sharpley (2000) said many developing countries are promoting tourism, because it offers the potential to create jobs, increase people's incomes and government revenues.

Moreover, besides providing benefits, there are also many negative impacts caused by tourism development. Inskeep (1991) mentioned that various types of environmental impacts caused by unplanned and thoughtless tourism development. Furthermore, Evita dkk. (2012), states that in fact, the economic benefits of tourism sector cause a problem in the depletion of natural resources, socio-cultural and environmental problems, as a result on the concept of tourism leading to mass tourism. The increasingly severe environmental damage has received a lot of criticism, thus, tourism development currently directed at alternative tourism that is more concerned to the environmental sustainability, it has done by implementing sustainable tourism such as Agrotourism development. On the other side, Utama (2011) said Agrotourism is an alternative tourism which is a massive solution in alleviating poverty. For this reason, the development of Agrotourism in Selingkar Wilis area is an option and effort to alleviate poverty. it is also supported by the economic potential of this area, one of which is Agrotourism.

Inside the research that has been done by Swastika (2017) the concerned variables are: government policies, entrepreneurship, infrastructure, agro-tourism development and community welfare. The relationship between these variables includes:
1. Positive and Significant, such as: (1) Government policies with entrepreneurship and infrastructure; (2) Entrepreneurship and Agrotourism development; (3) Infrastructure and Agrotourism development; (4) Agrotourism development and community welfare.

2. Positive and not significant, such as: (1) Government policies with Agrotourism development and community welfare; (2) *Entrepreneurship* with community welfare; (3) Infrastructure with community welfare.

Therefore, in the analysis by Swastika, indicates that the development of Agrotourism able to improve the community welfare, and to develop Agrotourism, government policies, entrepreneurship and infrastructure.

Pamulardi (2006) doing the research about the Development of Environmentally Friendly Agrotourism (Case Study on Tingkir Tourism Village, Salatiga) indicates that 1) Tingkir Lor Village has potential to be built and developed as an environmentally friendly Agrotourism location, at the same time it can help to develop Tingkir Tourism Village, which still cannot be called as tourist destination. 2) Community supports the development of tourism objects in Tingkir Tourism Village with the concept of environmentally friendly Agrotourism 3) Based on the seven steps of planning approach, ecotourism development model in Tingkir Tourism Village has purpose to develop agro cultivation as tourism object (attraction) that involve the community.

Based on the description above, it can be concluded that factors that influence the development of Potential Commodity-Based Agrotourism in Selingkar Wilis Area include: (1) the government role, (2) community participation, and (3) the attraction of Agrotourism development.

The study which more focuses on potential commodities, supports the mission of the Governor of East Java, Bhakti 6 : Jatim Agro, advancing the agricultural, livestock, fishery, forestry, plantation sectors to realize the welfare of farmers and fishermen, and Bhakti 7 Jatim Berdaya, efforts to strengthen the people's economy based on MSMEs through One Village One Product One Corporate and Agropolitan.

B. **Agropolitan**

Agropolitan is a concept based on the development of regional system which is able to facilitate the development of rural areas in strengthening rural-urban linkage. According to Anwar (2005), Agropolitan is a central place that has hierarchical structure, where agropolis means the existence of small and medium-sized cities around rural areas (micro urban-villages) that can grow and develop due to the functioning of coordination to the system of the main activities on agribusiness, and able to serve, encourage, attract, carry out agricultural development activities in the surrounding area. According to the Ministry of Forestry, agropolitan is an agricultural city that grows and develops and able to support the development of agribusiness systems therefore they can serve, encourage, attract, and promote agricultural development activities (agribusiness) in the surrounding area.

According to the Constitution number 26/2007, agropolitan area is an area consist of one or more activity that was done in rural areas as a system of agricultural production and management of certain natural resources. It is indicated by the existence of functional and hierarchical linkages to the settlement and agribusiness system. The agropolitan area is the embryo of an urban area which is oriented towards the development of agricultural activities, support activities, and product processing activities. The development of agropolitan areas is intended to improve the efficiency of infrastructure services and facilities for supporting agricultural activities, whether it requires before production, during the process of production, and after the process of production.

According to Government Regulation Number 15/2010, Article 72 paragraph (2) agropolitan areas needs to meet several criteria, including:

1. Agricultural rural areas that grow and develop due to the agribusiness systems and businesses that are able to serve, attract, and encourage agribusiness activities in the surrounding area.
2. Rural areas that have geomorphological, climatic, and topographical conditions that support agribusiness activities in agropolitan
3. Rural areas that have institutional support to develop agribusiness activities

1. The System of Agropolitan Area

    The agropolitan area is an area with 3 main sub-systems, such as: (1) main farmer town sub-system: concentrated service area accommodates external agribusiness relations, (2) farmer city sub-system: agribusiness service area, (3) hinterland sub-system: the area where agricultural production is carried out (on farm).

    Two sub-systems of the agropolitan area, consist of the main farmer's city and the farmer's city have components in form of infrastructure, superstructure, and supported by system mechanism facilitators (government, educators, researchers, communities). Like other urban areas, sub-system of the farmer's city and the main farmer's city has a part of city area that designated for residential areas, agro-industrial areas, and buffer zones. While in hinterland, there are sub protected areas and cultural areas. The agropolitan system area can be smoothly implemented when it is supported by supporting system (farmer economic institutions, financial/banking institutions, and other non-governmental organizations)

    Generally, Saragels and Krisnamurthi, in Suryanto, B (2004) said agribusiness system includes:
    a. The Upstream off-farm agribusiness sub-system contains industry economy activity that delivers

production facilities such as cattle breeds, feed production business, pharmaceutical industry, artificial insemination market, and others.
b. On-farm agribusiness sub-system is an economic activity called agricultural animal production to supply the primer farm product.
c. Downstream off-farm agribusiness sub-system is the activity of agro-industry process the primer farm product become processed products and trade of livestock product. This sub-system includes livestock slaughter procedures, the meat-canning industry, the leather industry, and the trade of export and import.
d. Supporting institution sub-system is the activity that provides service in farm agribusiness such as banking, transportation, counseling, peskesnak, holding ground, government policy (Farm Director General), educational institutions, and research (Saragih, 2000-2001).

Meanwhile, Hermawan, (2008 Page 4) stated that agribusiness consists of various sub-systems that relate to a series of interactions and a regular interdependence, and organizing in totality, with the five sub-systems are:
a. A sub-system of Provision of Production Facilities concerning procurement and distribution activities includes planning, management, technology, and resources so that the provision of production facilities or inputs for farming businesses meets the criteria on time, the right of quantity, type, quality, and product.
b. A farm sub-system or production process is an activity that includes coaching and development to increase the farm's primary production, in this example, site selection planning, commodities, technology, and farming patterns. It emphasizes

intensive farming and sustainability, which means increasing land productivity as much as possible with water and soil. Besides, it also emphasized farms in the commercial form, not as sub-system farms. The primary production will suit the market economy.

c. The agroindustry sub-system is the activity scope as simple processing at the farm level and as the whole activity from post-harvest handling at the advanced level. To add value to that primary product requires peeling, cleansing, milling, freezing, drying, and improving quality.

d. The marketing sub-system is the scope of market farm outcome and agroindustry for domestic market or export. The main activity is to monitor and develop market information on the domestic and export market.

e. The allowance subsystem is the activity of pre-harvest and post-harvest involves: production facilities and trade system, banking, extensions, agribusiness, farm groups, agribusiness infrastructure, agribusiness coop, BUMN, private, research and development, education, and training, transportation, government policy.

2. Area Typology

The central area of farm production has a typology that suits the classification of agricultural sub-sector and their *agro*-climatic requirements. It can be seen in the table below:

Tabel 1.1
Farm Area Typology

No.	Business Sector	Area Typology	Agroclimatic Requirements
1	Crops	The lowlands and highlands, with flat land textures, have adequate irrigation facilities.	It must be under the developed commodities, such as land height, soil type, land texture, climate, and soil acidity level.
2	Horticulture	Lowlands and highlands, with flat and hilly land textures and adequate water sources available	Must be following commodities types being developed, such as land height, soil type, land texture, climate, and soil acidity level.
3	Plantation	Highlands, with hilly land texture, close to land conservation areas.	Must be under the commodities type being developed, such as land height, soil type, land texture, climate, and soil acidity level.
4	Farm	Close to agricultural and plantation areas, with adequate sanitation systems.	The location should not be in a residential area and pay attention to aspects of environmental adaptation.
5	Inland Fishing	Inland fishing ponds, natural lakes, artificial lakes, and watersheds in cages and natural catchments.	Pay attention to ecological balance aspects and do not damage the existing environmental ecosystem.
6	Marine Fishing	Coastal areas to deep oceans within the boundaries of the Exclusive Economic Zone (EEZ).	Pay attention to aspects of ecological balance and do not damage the existing environmental ecosystem.

No.	Business Sector	Area Typology	Agroclimatic Requirements
7	Agrotourism	The development of agricultural and plantation businesses to continue to produce is developed into a natural tourism area without leaving its primary function as productive agricultural land.	Must be under the commodities type being developed, such as land height, soil type, land texture, climate, and soil acidity level.
8	Nature Conservation Tourism Forest	Protected forest area on state-owned land directly adjacent to agricultural and plantation land areas with clear boundary markings.	Following the characteristics of the natural environment of the local forest conservation area.

3. Criteria Determination of Leading Commodities

In the scope of Regency, the criteria for determining superior commodities refer to the criteria for superior national commodities. At the district level, essential commodities are divided into superior, mainstay, and potential commodities. According to agroecology, potential commodities are crop/livestock/fish commodities, where the current turnover is relatively low but has market opportunities. The mainstay commodity is a crop/livestock/fish commodity suitable for agroecology, where the current turnover is relatively high with good market opportunities but relatively not suitable for "positioning" or "trademark." Leading commodities are crops/livestock/fish commodities suitable for agroecology, where turnover is relatively high, market opportunities are good, and marketing can be used as a "positioning" or "trademark" tool. An area that can be developed into a food production center (*agropolitan*) area must meet the criteria for determining superior commodities as follows:

a. Based on potential local resource.
   These criteria count with finding the portion of imported raw material in leading plantation commodity (the data counted with the similar value of imported raw materials from the total volume/ quantity to produce the product). The more significant portion of imports of raw materials indicates a declining advantage.
b. Having a high opportunity to access the domestic market and the world
   The leading business sector must have a transparent market today and bright prospects in the future. In addition, to establish a development strategy, an obvious market for a plantation commodity will move farmers and entrepreneurs to commercialize plantation commodities. Hence, a linked market can direct a particular region to specialize so that inter-regional trade becomes one of the area drivers of economies in a particular region.
   The more significant number of plantation commodities will be marketed to show the ability to compete for these plantation commodities, because the share of the market business sector is getting higher. Concerning establishing a strategy for developing plantation commodities, this indicator is crucial for export promotion, import substitution, or meeting domestic needs. Generally, the market orientation groups into:
   a. Local market orientation within the district and the province
   b. Domestic market orientation is outside the province and inter-islands
   c. The export market orientation
      On the other hand, plantation commodities are generally for export promotion, so they have

a significant market orientation worldwide. Both within the framework of export promotion and import substitution, the size of the trade volume business sector greatly influences the regional economy, such as the opportunities for business and employment, linkages with sub-sectors, especially between the agricultural sector and industry, as well as trade and services in driving regional economy. The higher of trade volume, the higher role of these commodities in the regional economy.

c. Generating high added value

These criteria count based on the average annual growth of plantation commodities in one period. The higher the plantation commodity, the better the growth.

Technological support and reliable human resources determine the superiority of a plantation commodity. These supporting factors can stimulate business people to continue improving their results. Furthermore, actors will become more dynamic in business, processing results, trading, or other activities.

d. Eco-friendly

In order to generate better plantation commodities that can reduce costs or ecological damage, it is necessary to implement eco-friendly and clean technology, efficient agricultural waste usage, and good waste management. Production center areas that do not cause pollution and damage make the negative impact indicators smaller. The more significant negative impact occurs high cost because some funds are used for handling pollution and environmental damage.

e. Implement the principles of cooperation with a business orientation. This criterion reflects essential of cooperating with other parties if we want to develop this business so that we will not experience difficulties.
f. Administratively and economically feasible for business development. This criterion is essential because each established plantation commodity needs to be financially and economically so that entrepreneurs, investors, and the community are interested in working on these plantation commodities. Even though, it is a crucial plantation commodity, the government must cultivate it, if the plantation commodity is chosen with a low feasibility level. It is inefficient for the economy and state finances.

C. Tourism

Following the Law No.10 of 2009 tourism is called on Article one, such as:
1. Tourism is activity travel by individuals or groups to visit a particular place for recreation, private development, or to study an extraordinary tourist attraction in meantime.
2. Tourists are people who do tourism.
3. Tourism is supported by various facilities and services the community, entrepreneurs, government, and the local government provides.
4. Tourism is a multifaceted, interdisciplinary industry that reflects the needs of each individual and nation as well as interactions between travelers and communities, other travelers, the national government, local governments, and entrepreneurs.

5. The tourist attraction is the target tourist visit because it has uniqueness, beauty, and value in the form of a diversity of natural, cultural, and manufactured wealth.
6. A tourism destination is a geographical area that interrelated and complements the realization of tourism which located in one or more administrative tourist attractions, public facilities, tourism facilities, accessibility, and communities.
7. A tourism business is a work that provides goods and/or services to fulfill tourist needs and organize tourism.
8. A tourism Entrepreneur is a person or group who carries out tourism business activities.
9. The tourism industry is a collection of interrelated tourism businesses in producing goods and/or services to meet the tourists' needs in implementing tourism.
10. Strategic tourism areas have the primary function of tourism or the potential for tourism development, such as economic, social, and cultural growth, use of natural resources, environmental support, defense, and security.

D. Agrotourism

Agrotourism has been developed since the 20th century, where tourism is associated with the production environment of the agricultural sector (Zoto et al., 2013). Agrotourism explains as an activity related to tourism lessons for tourists to know better about the production process in the agricultural sector. They are making the agricultural area a place to enjoy the dishes of agricultural products directly.

According to Arifin (1992) agrotourism is one of the tourist acts done on farmland provides the beauty of nature on the farm, such as land preparation, planting, maintenance, harvesting, processing of harvested produce until ready for market and even tourists can buy these agricultural products as souvenirs. The agro-tourism involves tourists in agricultural activities. Meanwhile, Nurisjah (2001), agrotourism, wisata agro or farm tour was combining tourism and agricultural activities. Tirtawinata and Fachruddin (1996) stated that agrotourism was an effort to create new tourism products (diversification). The benefits of developing agro-tourism are increasing environmental conservation, aesthetic value, and natural beauty, providing recreational value, scientific activities, development, and economic profit (Tirtawinata and Fachruddin, 1999:30-43).

Agrotourism was a tourism development activity to increase an added value on agriculture and rural (Haeruman, 1989 in Khairul, 1997). Lobo et al. (1999) said that tourism development can create opportunities for local farmers to enhance their profit and living expenses. Therefore, the community's agricultural products have not been widely understood, so the actions of mediators often defeat farmers. This situation is very detrimental to farmers. The government should be able to help farmers to enjoy great benefits from agricultural products and groups farming. Supporting the development of agro-tourism, such as establishing cooperation with agreements that can provide mutual benefits.

It is causing an inconsistency in government to implement policy and a lack of attention in the local community, which induces some issues and hurdles. These issues can only be handled, if local society gives opportunities and enables actively in the development of tourism in the region, known as empowered (Pitana, 2011). Scheyvens (2002) stated that community empowerment can provide sustainable benefits for local communities.

Empowerment of the poor can be done by developing entrepreneurship in rural (Wahyudin, 2012). According to Zimmerer, entrepreneurship is a process of applying creativity and innovation so that can solve problems and find opportunities to improve lives (effort). Zimmerer et al. (2008) Also said, the biggest change faced by entrepreneurship nowadays is shifting world economies from modal-based financial to intellectual. Today, corporate intellectual capital is increasingly becoming a source of competitive advantage in the market.

As discussed in the previous chapter, In studying the economic development of potential commodity-based agro-tourism in the Selingkar Wilis area. These aspects are the focus study, which is internal and external factors, including (1) the government role, (2) community participation, and (3) the attractiveness of agro-tourism development.

1. Government Role

Damanik and Weber (2006) said the government role in developing the tourism such as: (1) assistance in tourism promotion, (2) business competition regulations and, (3) human resource development.

Claire A. Gunn (1988) emphasizes that several important aspects of regional policy function as very important tools in tourism planning. *First*, planning need to increase a quality growth, and changes that build, while the potential location expand to develop attraction quality that can be sold. *Second*, tourism policy has to play a more important role in promotion activity, and that policy needs to be supported by researchers. *Third*, tourism planning needs public cooperation so all stakeholders' hope can be fulfilled. *Fourth*, planning of regional policy and local have to amplify all schedules, supporting the good tourism development until destination level. *Fifth*, regional policy planning has to induce an effort to contribute to the construction area. *Sixth*, policies must connect businesses with the government and non-profit attractions. The travel company and other accommodations must support the planning policy of attraction business (nature and culture).

a. Accompanying of Tourism Promotion

In connects accompaniments of tourism promotion in Selingkar Wilis agrotourism development. It is related to some departments, such as Government Public Relations, Department of Information and Communications, Government Tourism Office, Department of Agriculture, and other institutions.

b. Competition Rules

In article 7 of Law Number 10 of 2009 concerning Tourism; there are four aspects of tourism development, including (a) the tourism industry, (b) tourism destinations, (c) marketing, and (d) tourism institutions, to build a good tourism business climate in the region.

c. SDM Development

Humans are a very important resource especially in service-based organizations, human resources manages a key role in realizing the successful performance (Evans, Campbell, & Stonehouse, 2003). Furthermore, tourism development was a critical role factor because tourism is a service industry. In the tourism industry, the company has an intangible, direct contact with consumers dependent on worker ability to evoke enthusiasm and create pleasure for every consumer (Setiawan, 2016: 23-24).

As mentioned earlier, in developing tourism human resources, they also pay attention to those four. The difference between human resources who work in a bureaucratic environment and tourism businesses to deal directly with tourists or are referred to as *frontliners*.

2. Society Participation

Participation means come with attention and donations given by participating groups in the community (Pasaribu, 1992). In developing and mobilizing the spirit of participation, the principles are needed to generate social power in society. Not only a community gathering in one particular place but also to hear explanations about what is prohibited from the speaker. Participation is a form of mental involvement/ thoughts and emotions or feelings in a group to contribute to achieving goals and responsibility for the business concerned (Keith Davis in Sastropoetro, 1998).

Three essential elements in Keith Davis' definition of participation require special attention: *first*, That participation is a mental and emotional attachment, more than words or physical involvement. *Second*, Availability contributes to achieve group goals; it means a sense of pleasure and volunteerism to help the group. *Third*, the element of responsibility. This element is a prominent aspect of the feeling of being a member. Recognized as a member means a sense of belonging (Sastropoetro, 1998). According to (Hermawan & Suryono, 2016) The stage of community participation is divided into four: planning, implementing, evaluating, and benefit taking.

To sum up the explanation above, society's participation in agrotourism development in Selingkir Wilis is the involvement of society in every development stage. It is through:

a. The involvement of emotions and feelings
b. Imparting a donation;
c. Sense of belongings.

a. The Involvement of Emotions and Feelings

This variable describes the condition of mental attachment and community feelings in planning, implementing, evaluating, and taking benefits of tourism development in the Selingkar Willis area.

b. Imparting a Donation

This variable describes the contribution made by the community in the planning, implementation,

evaluation, and benefit-taking of tourism development in the Selingkar Wilis area.
   c. Sense of Belongings
      This variable describes the community's sense of belonging in planning, implementation, evaluation, and benefit-taking of tourism development in Selingkar Wilis area.

3. Attraction of Agrotourism Development
   Globalization causes the competition in seizing the production factors to become sharper. The sharper competition sues the Regional Government to attract the investigation of people or industry in their area. The attraction of investigation on tourism, more to how the developing tourism in regional emphasized on tourism development to attract a person in the tourism field.
   According to Spillane, James J., (1995) The aspects of tourism planning include (1) Attraction. Can be classified into Site attraction is a permanent physical attraction with a permanent location in tourist destinations such as zoos, palaces, and museums. While an event attraction is an attraction that lasts temporarily, its location can be changed or moved fast, such as festivals, exhibitions, or regional art performances. (2) Facilities (necessary facilities). Facilities tend to be oriented towards attraction in a location because they must be close to the market. (3) Infrastructure. Fulfillment or the creation of infrastructure is a way to create a suitable atmosphere for tourism development. (4) Transportation. It determines the distance and time of a tourism trip. (5) Hospitality. The basic need for security and protection and the tenacity and friendliness

of the tourism workforce must be considered so that tourists feel safe and comfortable during their travels.

Meanwhile, Oka A. Yoeti. (1997) Aspects in tourism planning are (1) Tourists, (2) Transportation: how are the facilities available or to be used to carry tourists, (3) Tourist attraction (Attraction). Attractions to be sold must meet three conditions: (a) What can be seen (something to see), (b) What can be done (something to do), (c) What can be bought (something to buy) in DTW that on the visit; (4) service facilities; and (5) Information and promotions.

From the description above, it can conclude that the investment attractiveness of agro-tourism development includes the presence or availability in Selingkar Wilis : (a) Tourist, (b) Attraction, (c) Facilities, (d) Infrastructure, (e) Transportation, (f) Hospitality, and (g) Information and promotions.

a. *Tourist*

Tourists who visit the locus study become particular concern, as well as many visitors, tourism origin (domestic or international), visitors motif, social level, and others.

b. *Attraction*

Attraction is uniqueness, beauty, and value in the form of natural diversity, culture, and manufactured wealth as the target or tourist visits purpose. (Law No. 10 of 2009, concerning Tourism). Then, this study identifies the existence of tourist attractions, especially agro-tourism attractions at the study locus, starting from input (planting-picking), processing , to output (products).

c. *Facilities*

The tourism facilities refer to supporting facilities that create a sense of fun. It is accompanied by convenience and fulfillment of tourists' need in enjoying the products. For instance, the agro-tourism in Selingkar Wilis such as: homestay, food and beverage service, souvenir, public toilets and the others facilities.

d. *Infrastructure*

According to Sullivan, Arthur, and Steven M. S and Oxford Dictionary (2003), infrastructure refers to physical and social aspect. It can interpret as a basic biological need for organizing the structural system. It is used for public and private sector as service and facilities in improving the economic guarantees. Thus, those definition refers to technical and physical infrastructure that supports the provision such as roads, railways, clean water, airports, reservoirs, dams, waste management, electricity, telecommunications, and ports functionally. In this study there are several infrastructures includes road facilities, clean water, sanitation, telecommunications, electricity, and others.

e. *Transportation*

Yoeti (1997) stated that a good transportation service is a prerequisite for tourism development efforts. Particularly, it is for attracting the tourists to visit the tourism place. Therefore, it is not only focusing on quantity in this tourism transportation component. Nevertheless, quality, timeliness, comfort, and safety (such as: type, volume, tariff, and frequency of transportation capital to tourist areas) can assess the quality of transportation. Therefore, transportation in developing agro-tourism in the Selingkar Wilis area includes: the type, quantity, frequency and tariff of transportations that pass through the area.

f. *Hospitality.*

In developing the tourism, the hospitality become a crucial aspect to attract the tourist. It is particularly in improving the agrotourism in Selingkar Wilis. Thus, it will be the important consideration to tourist as the beneficial investment.

g. Information and Promotion

According to McLeod (2010:35), information is data that has been processed or has definition. In developing the agro-tourism in Selingkar Wilis, it conveys several characteristics such as relevance, accuracy, timeliness, and completeness. In addition, the information should implement tourism promotion.

Promotion is a marketing communication. Senjaya (1996) stated that communication is a process that involves four elements or components as follows: (1) The communicator or sender of the message; refers to a person or group, or organization that conveys the message. (2) Messages in the form of symbols or signs such as written or spoken words, pictures, numbers, and gestures. (3) Channel is used for delivering or sending messages e.g., telephone, radio, newspapers, magazines, TV, and airwaves in the context of face-to-face interpersonal communication. A person or group of people or organizations/institutions who are the target or recipient of the message. Besides the four elements mentioned above, there are three other essential factors in the communication process, namely: (1) Effects/impacts that occur on the recipient, (2) Feedback refers to the response from the recipient to the received message, (3)Noise, namely physical and psychological factors that can interfere or hinder the smooth communication process.

From the seven aspects of communication, the indicators of the variables in carrying out promotions' tourism include: (1) Accuracy in selecting information sources; (2) Accuracy in choosing messages; (3) Accuracy in choosing information media; (4) Accuracy in choosing message suggestions; (5) The suitability of the promotional response to its objectives; (6) The promotion has built tourism awareness and knowledge in the community; (7) The existence of alternative media promotion.

E. SWOT
1. The Definition of SWOT Analysis

    SWOT analysis is a strategic planning method used to evaluate Strengths, Weaknesses, Opportunities, and Threats in a project or business venture. It involves determining the objectives of the business venture. It is identifying excellent and favorable internal and external factors for achieving those goals. This technique was developed by Albert Humphrey, who led a research project at Stanford University in the 1960s and 1970s using data from Fortune 500 companies (Grewal & Levy, 2008).

    SWOT Analysis Theory is a theory that is used to strategic planning. SWOT is an abbreviation of Strength, Weakness, Opportunity, and Threat. SWOT is usually used to analyze a condition that will make a plan to carry out a work program (Buchari Alma, 2008).

2. Matrik SWOT

    The SWOT Matrix is an instrument to develop the strategic factor. It briefly describes the external threat and opportunity of the company. It will be accordance with the company's strength and weakness (Rangkuti, 2009). This matrix can produce four alternative and strategic possibility.

Tabel 1.2
Matrik SWOT

Internal Factors Analysis Summary (IFAS) / External Factors Analysis Summary (EFAS)	Strength (S) List 5-10 of Internal Factors	Weakness (W) List 5-10 of External Factors
Opportunity (O) List 5-10 of External Opportunity Factors	Strength opportunitiy (SO) The application of strength for utilizing the opportunity	Weakness Opportunity (WO) The application of weakness for utilizing the problem's opportunity
Threat (T) Daftarkan 5-10 List 5-10 of External Opportunity Factors	Strength Threat (ST) The application of strength for solving the threat	Weakness Threat (WT) This strategy used for minimalizing the weakness and avoiding the threat

Source: Rangkuti, 2004

Description:
1. SO Strategy

    This strategy based on the company's way of thinking. All strengths are used to seize and take the opportunity as significant as possible.
2. ST Strategy

    This strategy is based on how the company uses its strengths to overcome threats.
3. WO Strategy

    This strategy is implemented based on utilizing existing opportunities by minimizing existing weaknesses.
4. WT Strategy

    This strategy is based on defensive activities that try to minimize the company's weaknesses and avoid existing threats.

3. Accomplishment of a SWOT Matrix

In this section, we discussed how the company assessed the situation and reviewed the available corporate strategies. Then, identifying the ways or alternatives to use opportunities. It also to avoid threats and solve weaknesses.

According to Freddy Rangkuti (2005), SWOT is an identity of various factors to formulate service strategies systematically. It is based on the logic that can maximize opportunities and minimize weaknesses also the threats. To sum up, SWOT analysis compares the external and internal factors.

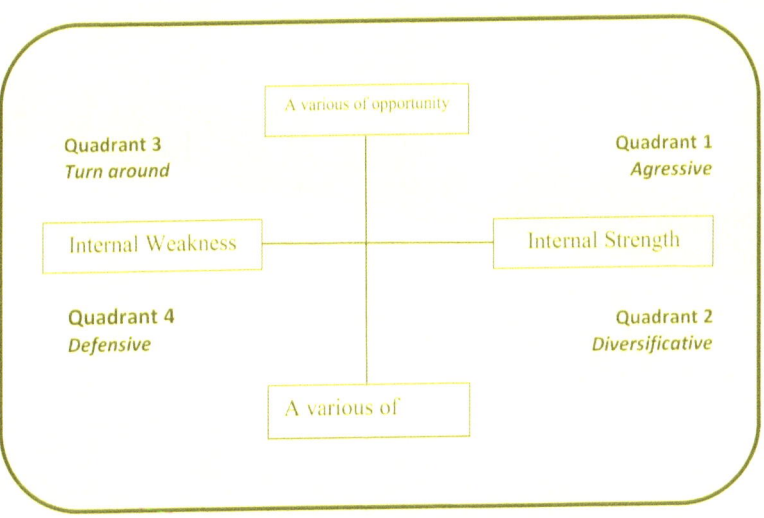

Figure 1.1.
SWOT Diagram
Sumber: Rangkuti (2009:19)

Description:

Quadrant 1 :
It is a very favorable situation. The company has opportunities and strengths to take advantage of current opportunities. The strategy that must be applied in this condition is to support an growth-oriented strategy.

Quadrant 2 :
Despite facing various threats, this company still has internal strength. The strategy must be applied to use strength to take advantage of long-term opportunities by employing a diversification strategy (product/service).

Quadrant 3 :
The company faces a significant market opportunity, but on the other hand, it faces several internal constraints/weaknesses. This company's focus is to minimize its internal problems so it can seize better market opportunities.

Quadrant 4 :
It is a very unfavorable situation. The company faces various internal threats and weaknesses.

4. Internality Externality (IE) Matrix

According to Rangkuti (2009: 42), "the internal and external matrices were developed from the General Electric (GE. Model)." The elements used include the parameters of the company's internal strength and external influences. The purpose of using this model is to obtain a more detailed corporate-level business strategy. The following is an IE matrix image that can model corporate strategy.

	Strength 3,00	Average 2,00	Weakness 1,00
High 3,00	1. GROWTH Concentration through vertical integration	2. GROWTH Concentration through horizontal integration	3. RETRENCHMENT *Turn around strategy*
Medium 2,00	4. STABILITY	5. GROWTH Concentration through horizontal integration	6. RETRENCHMENT Divestment Strategy
Low 1,00	8. GROWTH Concentric diversification	9. GROWTH Conglomerate Diversification	10. RETRENCHMENT Liquidation or Bankrupt

Figure 1.2
Internal and External Matrix (IE)
Source: Rangkuti (2009: 42)

Description:

1. *Growth strategy* is the growth of the company itself
2. *Stability strategy* adalah is a constant strategy; it is without changing the direction of the strategy.
3. *Retrenchement strategy* aims to minimize or reduce the effort made.

The detail explanation of IE Matrix strategy as follows:

1. Concentration through vertical integration can be achieved by taking over the function of the supplier or the distributor. It is the primary strategy of a company with a strong market position in a highly competitive industry.
2. The growth strategy through horizontal integration is to expand its product lines and distribution channels to other potential areas.
3. Turnaround Strategy is a strategy used to revive the company.

4. Divestment strategy is a strategy used to raise capital by selling non-earning assets and productive assets to be used to finance acquisitions or investments.
5. Concentric diversification is a growth strategy by making new products efficiently. Since the company already has good manufacturing and marketing capabilities.
6. Conglomerate diversification is a growth strategy through unrelated business activities. It can be carried out if the company confront a competitive position which is not really strong. Meanwhiel, the industry's attractiveness is very low. These two factors force the company to invest in other companies.
7. Liquidation strategy is a strategy that sells company assets that have real value.

CHAPTER II
ECONOMIC STUDY OF AGRO-TOURISM DEVELOPMENT BASED ON POTENTIAL COMMODITIES

A. Overview

According to the results of the Focus Group Discussion (FGD) with various related parties (Department of Tourism and Culture, Department of Community and Village Empowerment, Balitbang, Bapedalitbang, Department of Agriculture, Department of Public Works and Public Housing, and tourism community leaders both in agro-tourism areas, in general, the existing condition are The development of agro-tourism in Selingkar Wilis, as well as an overview of statistical data support,. It an be explained as follows; common problems found overtime during this study activity, both during visits to various agencies and during focus group discussions in Agrotourism Villages are as follows:
1. Accessibility is the main problem in developing tourism in the Selingkar Wilis area. It is because of the narrow road, up and down winding. In addition, the closeness of the residential area to the road; it is difficult to build the road. It may cause the low connectivity between regions in the Selingkar Wilis area. For instance, when

tourists visit the Selingkar Wilis area using a big bus, thus, it is difficult to be implemented.
2. Limitation of amenities to meet the tourists' necessary, the absence of rest areas, telecommunications networks, and public transportation.
3. There is agro-tourism is managed professionally. Durian, as one of the agro-tourism products, is still seasonal for a certain time.

Although it has significant problems developing Agrotourism in Selingkar Wilis, they become strengths and opportunities. It can be implemented by Presidential Decree No. 80 of 2019 concerning the Acceleration of Economic Development. The main problem in developing agro-tourism in Selingkar Wilis in the agro-tourism area is that this area is prone to landslides. Economic businesses that have the potential to develop to support agro-tourism are described as follows:

1. Agricultural Commodities

    Agricultural commodities in the Agropolitan area of Mojo and Semen sub-districts are rice, corn, cassava and peanuts. The existence of these agricultural commodities will support the development of agro-tourism as an added value for agricultural products

2. Horticulture
    a. Vegetables

        This commodities developed by the community in the Agropolitan Area include shallots, long beans, cucumbers, tomatoes, red chillies (large), green beans, cayenne pepper and petai. This horticultural commodity will benefit agro-tourism development in the Selingkar Wilis area. It will have the potential as educational tourism for picking vegetables.
    b. Fruit

        The fruit commodities are developed by the community in the Agropolitan Area: avocado, rambutan, guava, siam and large oranges, sapodilla, salak, melinjo, *duku/langsep*, mangosteen, durian, star fruit, soursop, mango, papaya, banana, jackfruit, cempedak, breadfruit and water guava.

c. Plantation

The production of plantation commodities in the Agropolitan area includes sugar cane, cocoa, coconut, coffee, cloves, cashew, *kapuk randu*, tobacco and patchouli.

d. Livestock

Livestock commodities in the Agropolitan Area include beef cattle, dairy cattle, buffalo, horses, goats and sheep, pigs, native chickens, laying hens, broilers, ducks and ducks and rabbits.

Particularly, related to the Dilem Wilis area, there is a A Review Preparation of Master Plan in the Dilem Wilis Land. The area of the Dilem Wilis tourist zone is approximately 132.29 hectares of blocks F and G. It has potential advantage that can be used for harvesting coffee and clove plants. Besides, the Dilem Wilis area can be developed as a tourist area with natural circumstances. For instance, the development and construction of a playground, camping ground, and supporting infrastructure. In addition, the water activities by stemming the flow of water in agro-tourism villages. It can attract tourists to the Dam. It is to increase the milk production into other derivative goods such as cheese, whole milk and others. The existing facilities that can be used and redeveloped are:

1. Lodging

The location and building of this inn already exist. However, for its future development, improvements are needed, both in the design of the building and its supporting facilities. It is

directed to be rest area for visitors with adequate facilities. Then, the modern building designs that can improve marketability and convenience for visitors.
2. Coffee Production Factory; historical heritage from the Dutch era
   The factory is near to the Dilem-Wilis development area. It is strongly supports the development of coffee production in the future, thus the development of Dilem-Wilis Agrotourism can be enjoyed and generate economic growth for the community.

3. Physical and land conditions support the development of plantation areas. Based on physical conditions, soil types and land in the Dilem-Wilis Agrotourism development area, several plantation crops that can be developed are coffee and cloves.
4. Nearby area: potential for dairy farming. In addition to developing plantation products and play tourism, the Dilem-Wilis Agrotourism area can also enjoy dairy farming products in pure milk. In the future, it is directed to develop dairy cow production, which can be in the form of a place to process milk into cheese and yoghurt.

In the Agrotourism Area, various facilities are heritage. In addition, there are also coffee production factories (machines), lodging, and umbrellas where visitors enjoy coffee and milk drinks provided by the Café.

The role and support of local governments such as policies, programs and activities that support the development of Potential Commodity-Based Agrotourism in Selingkar Wilis, Regional Regulation of Agrotourism Number 2 of 2020, concerning the Master Plan for Development of Agrotourism Village Tourism in 2019-2034. It is the government role and support in tourism development. The development of potential commodity-based agro-tourism is the development of a tourism destination. The Master Plan for Tourism Development states that district tourism development's objectives related to destinations are: (a) increasing the quality and quantity of tourism destinations; and (b) communicating district tourism destinations using various marketing media effectively, efficiently and responsibly.

The development of district tourism destinations (DPK), as referred to in this Regional Regulation, includes: (a) Regional DPK Development; (b) Development of Tourist Attractions; (c) Development of Tourism Accessibility; (d) Development of Public Infrastructure, Public Facilities and Tourism Facilities; (e) Community Empowerment through Tourism; and (f) Investment development in the tourism sector.

The DPK Development Territories include: (a) 3 (three) Regency Tourism Destinations (DPK); (b) 5 (five) Regency Tourism Strategic Areas (KSPK); and (c) 2 (two) Regency Tourism Development Areas (KPPK). Regency Tourism Destinations (DPK) are tourism destinations on a regency scale. Regency Tourism Strategic Areas (KSPKs) are the areas that have the main function of tourism or have the potential for the tourism. It has an important influence in several aspects such as economic, social and cultural growth; empowerment of natural resources, environmental carrying capacity, defence and security. Meanwhile, the Regency Tourism Development Area (KPPK) is a tourism area that has a tourism component and has a character or theme of certain tourism products. Those are dominant and strongly attached as a component of the image of the area.

DPK criteria include: (a) Having a geographical area with a district and cross-district and village area coverage in which there is a district tourism strategic area; (b) Having a quality tourist attraction that is widely known nationally and internationally; (c) Having the appropriateness of the theme of tourist attraction that supports the strengthening of competitiveness; (d) Having accessibility network and infrastructure that supports the movement of tourists and tourism activities; and (e) Having integration with related sector plans.

Meanwhile, the KSPK criteria include: (a) Having the main function of tourism or tourism development potential; (b) Having potential tourism resources to become a leading tourist attraction; (c) Having market potential, both nationally and especially internationally; (d) Has a potential position and role as an investor; (e) Having a strategic location that maintain the unity and integrity of the region; (f) Having a strategic function and role in maintaining the function and carrying capacity of the environment; (g) Having a strategic function and role in the preservation and utilization of cultural assets, including historical and archaeological aspects; (h) Having community readiness and support; (i) The specificity of the region; (j) Located in the main tourist market destination and national potential tourist market; and (k) Having the potential for future tourism product trends.

The indications of the Tourism Destinations program in the Selingkar Wilis Area is in line with the Regional Regulation Number 2, 2020. It is preparing a Master Plan and Detailed Plan for the Development of Regency Tourism Destinations and Regency Tourism Strategic Areas in the form of:

1. Prepare a Master Plan for the Development of Tourism Destinations for the Regency (DPK) of Mount Wilis and its surroundings with the theme of development based on Mountain Nature Tourism, Community-based Tourism (Tourism Village), Culture and Agrotourism.

2. Prepare a Building and Environmental Management Plan for Regency Tourism Attractions in the Gunung Wilis Regency Tourism Strategic Area (KSPK) and its surroundings with the theme of developing mountain nature-based tourism, community-based tourism (Tourism Village), Culture and Agrotourism.
3. Preparation of the Draft and Stipulation of the Regent's Regulation on the Master Plan of Kediri Regency Tourism Destinations (DPK) at Mount Wilis and its surroundings.
4. Preparation of the Draft and Stipulation of the Regent's Regulation on the Detailed Plan of the Gunung Wilis Regency Tourism Strategic Area (KSPK) and its surroundings.
5. Preparation of the Draft and Stipulation of the Regent's Regulation on Building and Environmental Management on Regency Tourist Attractions in the Regency Tourism Strategic Area (KSPK) of Gunung Wilis and its surroundings.
6. Dissemination of information and publication of the Regent's Regulation on the Development of Regency Tourism Destinations (DPK) at the foot of Mount Wilis and its surroundings.

In the Agropolitan Masterplan Review (2019), the Selingkar Wilis area is located in the Segobatam area. The vision of Segobatam's formulation is based on policy reviews such as the subdistrict and village in 2010-2030, Regency RPJPD in 2005-2025, and Regency RPJMD in 2016-2021. Based on these two aspects, it can be formulated that the vision of the Segobatam area is "Realizing the Segobatam Agropolitan Area Based on Superior Commodities of Mango and Oranges through the Development of Agricultural Technology and Improving the Quality of Human Resources."

The realization of the Segobatam agropolitan based on superior commodities of mango and orange is carried out by providing plant seeds for each commodity. The provision of plant seeds is made to reduce production costs. It is used by farmers in agricultural cultivation activities. In addition, the provision of plant seeds maintains the quality of agricultural products.

The development of the Segobatam area is also supported by the agricultural technology in processing agricultural products. The technology must have a sustainable element. It balance environmental, social and economic aspects. The development of agricultural technology is also accompanied by the quality of human resources. Efforts to improve the quality of human resources can be made by implementing outreach programs in the community and providing training on the management of agricultural products.

Based on the Segobatam's mission, it can be formulated as actions to achieve the vision. The missions of the agropolitan area of the Segobatam area such as: (1) Creating a centre and sub-centre of the Segobatam area that is integrated both in the agricultural and across sectors. (2) Provide seeds of superior commodities of mango and orange to reduce production costs. (3) Provide facilities and infrastructure to support agricultural cultivation activities. (4) Develop agricultural technology to support the process of agricultural. (5) Develop a marketing centre for agricultural and fishery products. (6) Conducting counselling and training on agricultural cultivation activities. (7) Develop tourism-based agropolitan areas by highlighting local commodities.

The spatial structure plan is prepared based on the location of the sub-district, which is the input and output of exclusive commodities; it has the potential to be developed. The determination of the spatial structure of the agropolitan area of the agro-tourism village. (1) Establishment of a system for agropolitan activities from upstream to downstream to marketing. (2) Improving the quality of seeding, processing, and production of only commodities such as organic rice and shallots. (3) Improvement of agropolitan facilities and infrastructure as a medium for developing only commodities. The determination and planning of the spatial structure of the agropolitan area are determined using several criteria, such as: (1) Agropolitan area of infrastructure facilities that function as supporting activities. (2) There is a relationship between the city and the village, and it has a reciprocal nature. (3) Dominating activities in a village, such as production, processing, and marketing. Mango and Orange Farming. An agricultural area is an agricultural activities consisting of seeding, cultivation, and processing activities.

1. Residential Area. It refers to farmers and residents who manage agriculture. The location of the distribution of settlements is around agricultural areas and industrial areas.
2. Facility. It supports facilities and public services that support agricultural activities, such as agricultural equipment shops, agricultural product storage warehouses, etc.
3. Processing industry. An industrial area is a process area of agricultural products.

This regulation explains that tourism destinations are geographical areas located in one or more administrative areas in which there are tourist attractions, public facilities, tourism facilities, accessibility and communities that are interrelated and complement the realization of tourism. Regional Tourism Destinations, abbreviated as DPD, are tourism destinations on a regional scale. Regional Tourism Strategic Areas, abbreviated as KSPD, are areas that have the primary function of tourism or have the potential for regional tourism development that has an important influence in one or more aspects such as economic, social and cultural growth, empowerment of natural resources, environmental carrying capacity and defence and security.

Regional Tourism Destination Development Territory is the result of regional tourism development, which is realized in regional tourism destinations and strategic areas. The development of DPD as referred to in this Regional Regulation includes: (a) Regional Development of DPD; (b) Development of Tourist Attractions; (c) Development of Tourism Accessibility; (d) Development of Public Infrastructure, Public Facilities and Tourism Facilities; (e) Community Empowerment through Tourism; and (f) Investment development in the tourism sector.

Regional Development DPD, as referred to in this Regional Regulation, includes DPD; and KSPD. The following criteria determine DPD: (a) It is a strategic area with regional or cross-district coverage or village in which there are areas for Regional Tourism Development, including KSPD; (b) Have a quality and widely known tourist attraction, nationally and internationally. It is a network of tourism products in the form of product packaging patterns and tourist visit patterns; (c) Having the appropriateness of the theme of Tourist Attraction that supports the strength of competitiveness; (d) Have accessibility network support and infrastructure that supports tourist movements and Tourism activities; and (e) Have integration with related sector plans.

Criteria determine KSPD; (a) The primary function of Tourism or tourism development potential; (b) Has potential tourism resources to become a leading tourist attraction and has a widely known image; (c) The market potential, both nationally and especially internationally; (d) The a potential position and role as an investment driver; (e) Having a strategic location that plays a role in maintaining the unity and integrity of the region; (f) Having a strategic function and role in maintaining the function and carrying capacity of the environment; (g) Having a strategic function and role in the preservation and utilization of cultural assets, including historical and archaeological aspects; (h) Have community readiness and support; (i) Has the specificity of the region; (j) Located in the leading tourist market destination and national potential tourist market; and (k) The potential for future tourism product trends.

The development of DPD and KSPD is carried out in stages with priority criteria having: (a) Destination components that are ready to be developed; (b) Effective position and role as a strategic investment attractor; (c) Strategic position as a systemic driving node for Tourism Development in the surrounding area, both in regional and national contexts; (d) Potential trends of future tourism products; (e) Significant contribution or positive prospects in attracting foreign and domestic tourists in a relatively short time; (f) widely known image; (g) Contribution to the development of tourism product diversity in the Region; and (h) International competitive advantage.

The policy directions for DPD and KSPD development include: (a) community-based DPD and KSPD Development Planning; (b) Enforcement of DPD and KSPD Development regulations; and (c) Controlling the implementation of DPD and KSPD development by prioritizing local wisdom. The strategy for planning DPD and KSPD development includes: (a) Preparing master plans and detailed plans for DPD and KSPD development; and (b) Formulating regulations on building and environmental arrangements for DPD and KSPD. The strategy for enforcing regulations on DPD and KSPD development is carried out through monitoring and supervision by local governments on the implementation of detailed plans for DPD and KSPD. The strategy for controlling the implementation of the DPD and KSPD Development plans. It is carried out through increased coordination between the government, regional governments, business actors, and the community. A Regent's Decree determines KSPD. The program indications in the Regional Regulation Number 26 of 2016 in Trenggalek Regency related to the development of Potential Commodity-Based Agrotourism in the Selingkar Wilis Area area:

1. Improve the availability of transportation modes (road, river, crossing, and sea transportation) to move tourists to and in Regional Tourism Destinations according to market needs and developments.
2. Improve the reliability of time and service schedules for transportation modes (road, river, ferry, sea, air, and rail) to support tourist travel patterns along main tourism corridors in national tourism destinations.
3. Development and improvement of infrastructure availability for transportation mode movement nodes (distribution centers and transportation gateways for road, river, ferry, and sea transportation) at strategic locations in regional tourism destinations according to market needs and developments.

The Master Plan for the Development of Agropolitan Areas: The realization of improving community welfare through agricultural revitalization, forestry, plantation-oriented agribusiness, food security, and environmentally friendly community empowerment. In order to realize the vision of the Dillem Wilis Gardens above, a mission as a work program is needed as follows:

1. Realizing the capabilities/skills of human resources, officials and farmers as well as optimizing the use of natural resources by taking into account environmental sustainability;
2. Realizing technology transfer, increasing food security and partnerships

3. Realizing and ensuring the existence and use of plantation resources wisely and professionally with an industrial culture based on efficiency, productivity, and sustainability with efforts to improve the traditional plantation system for the dignity and benefits of the perpetrators.
4. Implementing technical programs and policies, fostering, controlling, monitoring, or evaluating food and society availability.

The Planning of Agro-tourism Village Garden Tourist Attractions that will be developed includes:
1. Integrated Animal Husbandry Educational Tourism Planning
2. Planning of Flower Garden Cultivation Area, Rare Plants, and Ornamental Plants
3. Terrace Agricultural Tourism Area Planning
4. Planning of the Agrotourism Village Coffee Processing Factory Museum
5. Planning of Agrotourism Village Garden History Museum
6. Riverside Rest Area Plan
7. Peak Monitoring Area Planning
8. Outbound Field Area
9. ATV Circuit Arena Plan
10. Flying Fox Area Planning
11. Natural Swimming Pool Area Plan
12. Mini Reservoir Tourism Area Plan (Embung) Agrotourism Village
13. Body Rafting Track Plan

Cluster Plan for Development of Agro-tourism Areas, including:
1. Agrotourism Education Cluster Plan for Agro-tourism Village Gardens;
2. Historical and Recreational Tourism Cluster Plan;
3. Play Zone and Agility Zone Cluster Plans;
4. Water Tourism Cluster Plan.

The Agrotourism Village Garden Infrastructure Development Plan are:
1. Road Access and Street Lighting;
2. Plans for Entrance Gate to Agrotourism Areas;
3. Open Space and Parking Area Plans;
4. Tourist Route Plans and Visitor Transportation;
5. Lodging and Homestay Plans;
6. Plan for Provision of Clean Water Needs;
7. Sanitation and Solid Waste;
8. Community Trading Area Plan.

The Community Synergy Plan is that synergies with the community around the Agrotourism Village plantation can be carried out by creating community-based activity programs. In these activities, the community can independently carry out activities that support agrotourism activities in the Agrotourism Village Garden. Synergy activities that need to be carried out are:
1. The community participates in managing homestays and lodges
2. The community participates in terracing agricultural tourism attractions and becomes a mentor for tourists.
3. The community participates in the process of providing accommodation and transportation for tourists
4. The community is involved in managing the cleanliness of the agrotourism area as a task force or community group managing TPST
5. The community establishes SMEs that produce souvenirs
6. Building a trading area, as a support for selling SME products, so that it becomes an opportunity for economic improvement activities in the Agrotourism Village Garden.

The Agrotourism Village Garden Infrastructure Development Plan are:
1. Road Access and Street Lighting;
2. Plans for Entrance Gate to Agrotourism Areas;

3. Open Space and Parking Area Plans;
4. Tourist Route Plans and Visitor Transportation;
5. Lodging and Homestay Plans;
6. Plan for Provision of Clean Water Needs;
7. Sanitation and Solid Waste;
8. Community Trading Area Plan.

The Community Synergy Plan is that synergies with the community around the Agrotourism Village plantation can be carried out by creating community-based activity programs. In these activities, the community can independently carry out activities that support agrotourism activities in the Agrotourism Village Garden. Synergy activities that need to be carried out are:

1. The community participates in managing homestays and lodges
2. The community participates in terracing agricultural tourism attractions and becomes a mentor for tourists.
3. The community participates in the process of providing accommodation and transportation for tourists
4. The community is involved in managing the cleanliness of the agrotourism area as a task force or community group managing TPST
5. The community establishes SMEs that produce souvenirs
6. Building a trading area, as a support for selling SME products, so that it becomes an opportunity for economic improvement activities in the Agrotourism Village Garden.

CHAPTER III
POTENTIAL BUSINESS ACTIVITIES IN AGROTOURISM DEVELOPMENT

With an area of 18,675 hectares of agricultural land in the Agropolitan Area in the Agrotourism area, the commodities owned include: agricultural commodities; horticultural commodities; plantation commodities and livestock commodities. (1) Agricultural commodities in the Agropolitan Area of Mojo and Semen Sub Districts are: rice, corn, cassava and peanuts. (2) Horticultural commodities (a) Vegetables are: shallots, long beans, cucumbers, tomatoes, red chilies (large), green beans, cayenne pepper and petai. (b) Fruits are: avocado, rambutan, guava, siam and large oranges, sapodilla, salak, melinjo, duku/langsep, mangosteen, durian, star fruit, soursop, mango, papaya, banana, jackfruit/champedak, breadfruit and guava. (3) Plantation commodities in the Agropolitan area include: sugar cane, cocoa, coconut, coffee, cloves, cashew, kapok, ylang, tobacco and patchouli. (4) Livestock commodities in the Agropolitan Area of Mojo and Semen Sub Districts include: beef cattle, dairy cattle, buffalo, horses, goats and sheep, pigs, free-range chickens, laying hens, broilers, ducks and ducks and rabbits.

In addition, the agro-tourism village also has several production sites, including: (1) Production of food ingredients, namely: lowland rice, upland rice, corn, cassava, sweet potatoes, peanuts, and soybeans. (2) Vegetable production consists of Spinach, Green Chillies, Chili Peppers, Cayenne Pepper, Potatoes, Kangkung, Long Beans, Labusiam, Beans, Young Jackfruit, Petai, Petcai / mustard greens, Tomatoes, and Eggplants. (3) Fruit production in Bendungan District consists of Avocado, Durian, Guava, Mango, Mangosteen, Jackfruit, Papaya, Banana, Rambutan, Salak, Soursop, and Breadfruit. And (4) Biopharmaceutical plants consist of ginger, kencur, turmeric, noni, galangal, temu ireng, temu lock, temu comedy, and lempuyang.

A. Role/Support of Local Government

The role and support of local governments in the development of potential commodity-based agro-tourism in Agro-tourism Villages are as follows;

The most significant role of local governments in the development of potential commodity-based agro-tourism in the Agro-tourism Village Area is the existence of the Master Plan for Tourism Development in agro-tourism villages 2019-2034 which is outlined in the form of Regional Regulation Number 2 of 2020. The Selingkar Wilis area on the Kediri Regency side is in a Strategic Area Tourism (KSPK) of Mount Wilis and its surroundings, which includes the sub-districts of: Semen, Grogol, Banyakan, Tarokan, and Mojo (Segobatam).

The indications of the Tourism Destinations program in the Selingkar Wilis Area according to Regional Regulation Number 2, 2020 include: (1) Preparing a Master Plan for the Development of Regency Tourism Destinations (DPK) at the foot of Mount Wilis and its surroundings with the theme of development based on Mountain Nature Tourism, Community-based Tourism (Tourism Village), Culture and Agrotourism; (2) Prepare a Building and Environmental Management Plan for Regency Tourism Attractions in the Regency Tourism Strategic Area (KSPK) of Gunung Wilis and its surroundings with the theme of development based on mountainous nature tourism, community-based tourism (Tourism Village), Culture and Agrotourism; (3) Preparation of the Draft and Stipulation of the Regent's Regulation concerning the Master Plan for the Regency Tourism Destinations (DPK) at the foot of Mount Wilis and its surroundings; (4) Preparation of the Draft and Stipulation of the Regent's Regulation concerning the Detailed Plan for the Tourism Strategic Area of the Regency (KSPK) of Gunung Wilis and its surroundings; (5) Preparation of the Draft and Stipulation of the Regent's Regulation on Building and Environmental Management on Regency Tourist Attractions in the Regency Tourism Strategic Area (KSPK) of Gunung Wilis and its surroundings; (6) Dissemination of information and publication of the Regent's Regulation on the Development of Tourism Destinations for the District (DPK) at the foot of Mount Wilis and its surroundings.

Another government role after the Master Plan for Tourism Development in Kediri Regency 2019-2034 is the Review of the Agropolitan Village Agrotourism Master Plan (2019), with the vision of "Realizing the Segobatam Agropolitan Area Based on Superior Commodities of Mango and Orange Through Agricultural Technology Development and Improvement of the Quality of Human Resources". The missions of the agropolitan area of the Segobatam area include: (1) Creating regional centers and sub-centers that are integrated with the agricultural sector and across sectors. (2) Provide seeds of superior commodities of mango and orange in order to reduce production costs. (3) Provide facilities and infrastructure to support agricultural cultivation activities. (4) Develop agricultural technology to support agricultural product processing activities. (5) Develop a marketing center for agricultural and fishery products. (6) Conducting counseling and training on agricultural cultivation activities. (7) Develop tourism-based agropolitan areas by highlighting local commodities. Determination of the spatial structure of the agropolitan area of Kediri Regency has the following objectives. (1) Establishment of a system for agropolitan activities from upstream to downstream to marketing. (2) Improving the quality of seeding, processing, and production of superior commodities such as organic rice and shallots. (3) Improvement of agropolitan facilities and infrastructure that functions as a medium for developing superior commodities.

The form of the development of the Dillem Wilis Gardens is in the form of a mission as a work program in the form of: (1) Realizing the capabilities/skills of human resources, officials and farmers as well as optimizing the use of natural resources by paying attention to environmental sustainability; (2) Realizing technology transfer, increasing food security and partnerships; (3) Realizing and ensuring the existence and use of plantation resources wisely and professionally with industrial culture on the basis of efficiency, productivity and sustainability with efforts to improve the traditional plantation system for the dignity and benefits of the perpetrators; (4) Implementing technical programs and policies, fostering, controlling, monitoring or evaluating food availability, food distribution, food consumption, food awareness and community empowerment; and (5) Planning for Dillem Wilis Gardens Attractions Attractions which include: (a) Integrated Animal Husbandry Educational Tourism Planning; (b) Planning of Flower Garden Cultivation Area, Rare Plants and Ornamental Plants; (c) Terrace Agricultural Tourism Area Planning; (d) Planning for the Van Dillem Coffee Processing Factory Museum; (e) Planning of the Dillem Wilis Garden History Museum; (f) Riverside Rest Area Plan; (g) Peak Monitoring Area Planning; (h) Outbound Field Area; (i) ATV Circuit Arena Plans; (j) Flying Fox Area Planning; (k) Natural Swimming Pool Area Plan; (l) Dillem Wilis Mini Reservoir (Embung) Tourism Area Plan; (m) Planned Body Rafting

Track. Cluster Plan for Development of Agro-tourism Areas, which includes: (1) Cluster Plan for Educational Agro-tourism at Dillem Wilis Gardens; (2) Historical and Recreational Tourism Cluster Plan; (3) Play Zone and Agility Zone Cluster Plans; (4) Water Tourism Cluster Plan. The Dillem Wilis Plantation Infrastructure Development Plan includes the development of: (1) Road Access and Street Lighting; (2) Plan for Entrance Gate to Agrotourism Areas; (3) Open Space and Parking Area Plans; (4) Tourist Route Plans and Visitor Transportation; (5) Lodging and HomeStay Plans; (6) Plan for Provision of Clean Water Needs; (7) Sanitation and Solid Waste; (8) Community Trading Area Plan.

The Community Synergy Plan is to synergize with the community around the Dillem Wilis plantation with activities in the form of: (1) The community participates in managing *homestays* and tourist lodges; (2) The community participates in terracing agricultural tourism attractions and becomes a mentor for tourists; (3) The community participates in the process of providing accommodation and transportation for tourists; (4) The community is involved in managing the cleanliness of the agro-tourism area as a task force or community group managing the TPST; (5) The community establishes SMEs that produce souvenirs and souvenirs; (6) Building a trading area, as a support for selling SME products, so that it becomes an opportunity for economic improvement activities in the Dillem Wilis Plantation.

Other activities are developing Tourism Villages that have potential: natural beauty and plantations, livestock and historical heritage, as well as having natural tourist attractions, including waterfalls, Dilem Wilis plantations, productive forests that are quite varied from Pine, Mahogany and so on.

B. **Analysis of Internal Factors (Strengths and Weaknesses) and External Factors (Opportunities and Obstacles)**

As mentioned in chapter 3.4 that the stages in the SWOT operational framework, the stages include: (1) Identification of internal and external factors; (2) the weighting and ranking of several influencing variables; (3) Making conclusions and selecting strategies; and (4) Realizing the strategy in an action.

1. Identification of Internal and External Factors

    This stage is to identify and separate the variables of strength and weakness in internal factors, and opportunities and threats in external factors,

Internal
Strength
a. Government Role:
   1) Promotional assistance
      a) The involvement of all tourism promotion institutions in tourism promotion (Department of Communication and Informatics, Public Relations Section, Department of Tourism, Department of Agriculture, Department of Community and Village Empowerment.
      b) Precisely the selection of information media and the target of agrotourism promotion messages
   2) Competition Regulations

      The existence of competition regulations that provide space for the development of the tourism industry and tourism marketing
   3) HR Development
      a) The development of bureaucratic human resources has been and is being carried out to support the development of the tourism industry, tourism destinations, and tourism marketing

b) The development of frontliner human resources has been and is being carried out to support the development of the tourism industry, tourism destinations, tourism marketing, and tourism institutions.
b. **The Attractiveness of Agrotourism Development**
1) Traveler. The number of domestic tourist visits in the agro-tourism area
2) Tourist attraction. The amount of potential for planting-picking agro-tourism and agrotourism production results
3) Facility. There are a sufficient number of places to eat and drink, places for souvenirs and gazebos for resting.
4) Infrastructure
   a) There is clean water in sufficient quantity, organized and clean water quality that meets health standards.
   b) There is electricity supply in all areas.
5) Transportation. There are transportation services: (1) with frequent frequency, (2) sufficient transport capacity, (3) reasonable fares, and (4) safe and comfortable in agrotourism areas.

Weaknesses
a. **Role of Government:**
1) Promotional assistance. There is no or lack of accuracy in choosing agrotourism promotional content and the suitability of agrotourism promotion responses with their goals.
2) Competition regulations. The absence or lack of competition regulations that provide space for the development of tourism destinations and tourism institutions.

3) HR Development. The development of bureaucratic human resources has not been or has not been carried out to support the development of tourism institutions.
b. **The Attractiveness of Agro-tourism Development**
   1) Traveler. Not many foreign tourist visits.
   2) Tourist attraction. (1) There is no agro-tourism in the production process. (2) Regional finance has not provided an adequate portion for the development of agro-tourism and there is legal certainty that encourages the development of agrotourism.
c. **Facilities**
   There are not enough lodging (*homestay*) and public toilets.
d. **Infrastructure**
   1) The unavailability of the main road to enter an adequate area, traversed village roads, and safe and comfortable footpaths
   2) There is not yet a good telecommunication signal and sufficient telecommunication credit outlets/sellers
e. **Transportation**
   There are no various types of transportation services in the agrotourism area

Opportunity
a. **Community Participation**
   1) Mental Attachments and Feelings. The community has a mental attachment and feeling in the implementation of development.
   2) Make donations; (1) The community contributes (material and immaterial) in the implementation of development. (2) The community makes optimal use of the results of development.

3) A sense of belonging. The community is responsible for the preparation of development planning, implementation of development, and evaluation of agrotourism development

b. **The Attractiveness of Agrotourism Development**
   1) Community Engagement and Benefits
      a) Communities around the agrotourism area care about visiting tourists
      b) Communities around the agrotourism area get economic benefits by improving the quality of their products (added value).
      c) Communities around the agro-tourism area get economic benefits by increasing their income
   2) Information and Promotion
      a) It is easy for tourists to get correct information related to what is in the agrotourism area.
      b) Promotion is carried out with sufficient regard to the location and potential of agro-tourism
   3) The Role of Tourism Organizations. The Indonesian Hotel and Restaurant Association (PHRI) and the Indonesian Agrotourism Association (AWAI) have or will play an active role in the development of agro-tourism in Selingkar Wilis.
   4) Role and Contribution of Agrotourism Management
      a) Selingkar Wilis is an economically attractive area to develop agro-tourism business
      b) The development of agro-tourism in Selingkar Wilis will increase the knowledge of the people around

Threat
a. **Community Participation**
   1) Mental Attachments and Feelings. The community does not yet have a mental attachment and feeling in the preparation of development planning,

implementation of development evaluation and utilization of development results.
2) Make a donation. The community has not contributed (material and immaterial) in the preparation of development planning and development evaluation.
3) A sense of belonging. The community has not been responsible for the implementation of the utilization of the results of agrotourism development.

b. The Attractiveness of Agro-tourism Development
1) Community Engagement and Benefits. Communities around the agrotourism area are friendly to tourists who visit
2) The Role of Tourism Organizations. The tourism entrepreneur association (ASITA) and the Indonesian tour guide Association (HPI) have not yet played an active role in the development of agrotourism in Selingkar Wilis
3) Role and Contribution of Agrotourism Management
   a) Downstreaming of agricultural products has not been carried out in the Selingkar Wilis area by agrotourism managers.
   b) Empowerment of local communities has not been carried out in the development of agrotourism in Selingkar Wilis by agrotourism managers.
   c) In the development of agrotourism, the Selingkar Wilis area has not been considered *marketable* (has a potential market) by agrotourism managers.

External
Strength Factors
a. Government Role
   1) Promotional assistance. (1) There is involvement of all tourism promotion institutions in tourism

promotion (Kominfo Service, Public Relations Division, Tourism Office, Agriculture Service, Community and Village Empowerment Service). (2) Accuracy in selecting agrotourism promotion information media.
   2) Competition regulations. The existence of competition regulations that provide space for the development of the tourism industry and tourism institutions.
   3) HR Development
      a) The development of bureaucratic human resources has been and is being carried out to support the development of the tourism industry and tourism institutions.
      b) The development of frontliner human resources has been and is being carried out to support the development of tourism destinations, tourism marketing and tourism institutions.
b. **The Attractiveness of Agro-tourism Development**
   1) Traveler. The number of domestic tourists visiting the agrotourism area
   2) Tourist Attractions
      a) The number of agrotourism products produced
      b) Regional finance that provides an adequate portion for the development of agrotourism
      c) The existence of legal certainty that encourages the development of agrotourism
   3) Facility. There are a sufficient number of places to eat and drink, places for souvenirs, public toilets, and gazebos for resting in the agrotourism area.
   4) Infrastructure
      a) There is clean water in sufficient and organized quantity, as well as clean water quality that meets health standards
      b) There is electricity supply in all areas

5) Transportation. There are transportation services with sufficient carrying capacity, reasonable fares, and safe and comfortable transportation in the agrotourism area.

Weaknesses
a. **Government Role**
   1) Promotional assistance
      a) Not yet precise in choosing agrotourism promotional content and in choosing the target of agro-tourism promotion messages.
      b) The response to agro-tourism promotion is not yet matched with its objectives
   2) Competition regulations. There are not enough competition regulations that provide space for the development of tourism destinations and tourism marketing.
   3) HR Development
      a) The development of bureaucratic human resources has not been optimally carried out to support the development of tourism destinations and tourism marketing.
      b) The development of frontliner human resources has not been optimally carried out to support the development of the tourism industry.
b. **The Attractiveness of Agrotourism Development**
   1) Traveler. Not many foreign tourists visit
   2) Tourist attraction. There is not much potential for planting-picking agrotourism and agrotourism in the production process
   3) Facility. There are not enough lodgings (homestays)
   4) Infrastructure
      a) There is no main road to enter an adequate area, easy village roads, and comfortable and safe footpaths.

b) The unavailability of good telecommunication signals and sufficient telecommunication credit outlets/sellers.
  c. **Transportation**
   1) There are no various types of transportation services in the agrotourism area.
   2) There is no transportation service with a frequent frequency in the agrotourism area.

Opportunity
a. **Community Participation**
   1) Mental Attachments and Feelings. The community has a mental attachment and feeling in utilizing the results of development.
   2) Make a donation. Communities make optimal use of the results of development.
   3) A sense of belonging. The community is responsible for the preparation of agrotourism development planning, the implementation of agrotourism development and the implementation of the utilization of the results of agrotourism development.
b. **The Attractiveness of Agrotourism Development**
   1) Community Engagement and Benefits. Communities around the agrotourism area are friendly to visiting tourists, care about visiting tourists and get economic benefits by increasing their income.
   2) Information and Promotion
      a) It is easy for tourists to get correct information related to what is in the agrotourism area.
      b) Promotion is carried out with sufficient regard to the location and potential of agrotourism.
   3) The Role of Tourism Organizations. The Indonesian Hotel and Restaurant Association (PHRI) and the Indonesian Agrotourism Association (AWAI) have

or will play an active role in the development of agrotourism in Selingkar Wilis.
4) Role and Contribution of Agro Tourism Management
   a) Selingkar Wilis is an economically attractive area to develop agrotourism business.
   b) The development of agrotourism in Selingkar Wilis will increase the knowledge of the surrounding community.

Threat (Obstacles)
a. Community Participation
   1) Mental Attachments and Feelings. There is no mental attachment and feeling in the preparation of planning, implementation, and evaluation of development by the community.
   2) Make a donation. The community has not contributed (material and immaterial) in the preparation of development planning, implementation of development and implementation of development evaluation.
   3) A sense of belonging. The community has not participated and is responsible for the evaluation of agro-tourism development.
b. The Attractiveness of Agrotourism Development
   1) Community Engagement and Benefits. Communities around the agro-tourism area have not felt that they have received economic benefits by increasing the quality of their products (*added value*).
   2) The Role of Tourism Organizations. The Association of Tourism Entrepreneurs (ASITA) and the Association of Indonesian Tour Guides (HPI) have not yet played an active role in the development of agro-tourism in Selingkar Wilis.

3) Role and Contribution of Agro Tourism Management
   a) Downstreaming of agricultural products has not been optimally carried out in the Selingkar Wilis area.
   b) Empowerment of local communities has not been optimally carried out in the development of agro-tourism in Selingkar Wilis.
   c) In the development of agrotourism, Selingkar Wilis is not considered a *marketable* (has a potential market).

2. Weighting and Ranking of Variables The
   Weighting and ranking of several influencing variables is then converted into a matrix so that it can determine the position of an organization or company in which quadrant.

Table 3.1
Weighting and Ranking of Internal Variable Agrotourism Study

NO	INTERNAL FACTOR	FREQUENCY	WEIGHT	RATING	SCORE
	STRENGTH				
1	The involvement of all PEMDA's institutions in tourism promotion. (1)	61	0.029	4.06	0.118
2	The consistency in choosing agrotourism promotion content. (2)	53	0.025	3.53	0.088
3	The consistency in choosing tourism information and promotion media. (3)	63	0.030	4.20	0.126

NO	INTERNAL FACTOR	FREQUENCY	WEIGHT	RATING	SCORE
4	The consistency in choosing the marketing target of agrotourim promotion. (4)	59	0.028	3.93	0.110
5	The compatibility between agrotourism promotion responses and its target. (5)	58	0.027	3.86	0.104
6	The presence of regulation that give space for tourism industry to develop. (6)	55	0.026	3.66	0.095
7	The presence of regulation that give space for tourism marketing to develop. (8)	55	0.026	3.66	0.095
8	The presence of regulation that give space for tourism institution to develop. (9)	53	0.025	3.53	0.088
9	The bureaucracy of human resources to support the development of tourism industry. (10)	56	0.026	3.73	0.097
10	The bureaucracy of human resources to support the development of tourism destinations. (11)	56	0.026	3.73	0.097
11	The bureaucracy of human resources to support the development of tourism marketing. (12)	58	0.027	3.86	0.104
12	The bureaucracy of human resources to support the development of tourism institutions. (13)	54	0.025	3.60	0.090

The Development of Potential Commodity-Based Agrotourism

NO	INTERNAL FACTOR	FREQUENCY	WEIGHT	RATING	SCORE
13	The frontliner of human resources in supporting the tourism industry development. (14)	50	0.024	3.33	0.080
14	The frontliner of human resources in supporting the tourism destinations development. (15)	50	0.024	3.33	0.080
15	The frontliner of human resources in supporting tourism marketing development.(16)	50	0.024	3.33	0.080
16	The frontliner of human resources in supporting tourism institutional. (17)	50	0.024	3.33	0.080
17	The numbers of domestic tourist visitor in study locus.(18)	59	0.028	3.93	0.110
18	The number of "tanam-petik" / pick and plant agrotourism potensial. (20)	55	0.026	3.66	0.095
19	The number of agrotourism production result. (22)	51	0.024	3.40	0.081
20	The sufficient number of food courts. (26)	54	0.025	3.60	0.090
21	The sufficient number of souvenir stores. (27)	52	0.024	3.46	0.083
22	The comfort and safe walk path. (32)	51	0.024	3.40	0.081
23	The sufficient and organized number of clean water. (33)	51	0.024	3.40	0.081
24	The quality of clean water that meet the health standard. (34)	53	0.025	3.53	0.088
25	The sufficient number of electricity sources in each area. (35)	57	0.027	3.80	0.102

NO	INTERNAL FACTOR	FREQUENCY	WEIGHT	RATING	SCORE
	WEAKNESS				2,343
1	There is regulation that give space for tourism destination development. (7)	42	0.020	2.80	0.056
2	The number of foreign tourist visitors. (19)	36	0.017	2.40	0.040
3	The number of agrotourism production process. (21)	44	0.021	2.93	0.061
4	The regional financial give sufficient portion for agrotourism development. (23)	44	0.021	2.93	0.061
5	There is legal certainty to push the agrotourism development. (24)	44	0.021	2.93	0.061
6	There is sufficient number of inn/lodging. (25)	33	0.016	2.20	0.035
7	There is sufficient number of public toilet. (28)	36	0.017	2.40	0.040
8	There is sufficient number of gazebo/rest area. (29)	46	0.022	3.06	0.067
9	The adequate main enterance area. (30)	47	0.022	3.13	0.069
10	The road that easy to be accessed. (31)	49	0.023	3.26	0.075
11	There is a good telecommunication signal. (36)	48	0.023	3.20	0.073
12	There is enough telecommunication credit outlets/sellers. (37)	48	0.023	3.20	0.073
13	There are various types of transportation services in agrotourism area. (38)	40	0.019	2.66	0.051

NO	INTERNAL FACTOR	FREQUENCY	WEIGHT	RATING	SCORE
14	Frequent transportation service agrotourism area. (39)	42	0.020	2.80	0.056
15	There is transportation service with enough carrying capacity in agrotourism area. (40)	42	0.020	2.80	0.056
16	There is transportation service with decent rate in agrotourism area. (41)	42	0.020	2.80	0.056
17	Safe and comfortable transportation service in agrotourism area. (42)	42	0.020	2.80	0.056
					0.986
			TOTAL	2,343 + 0,986	3.329

Table 3.2
Weighting and Ranking External Variable of Agrotourism Study

NO	EXTERNAL FACTOR	FREQUENCY	WEIGHT	RATING	SCORE
	OPPORTUNITY				
1	Have mental and emotional connection in the preparation of development planning. (1)	54	0.036	3.60	0.129
2	Have mental and emotional connection in the implementation of development. (2)	55	0.037	3.66	0.135
3	Responsible on the arrangement of agrotourism development planning. (9)	54	0.036	3.60	0.129

NO	EXTERNAL FACTOR	FREQUENCY	WEIGHT	RATING	SCORE
4	Responsible on the implementation of agrotourism development. (10)	54	0.036	3.60	0.129
5	Responsible on the implementation of agrotourism development evaluation. (11)	54	0.036	3.60	0.129
6	The society around the agrotourism area is kind to the tourists visitor. (13)	61	0.041	4.06	0.166
7	The society around the agrotourism area is care to the tourists visitor. (14)	61	0.041	4.06	0.166
8	The society gets economy benefit by enhancing the product quality (added value). (15)	63	0.042	4.20	0.176
9	The society gets economy benefit by enhancing their income. (16)	63	0.042	4.20	0.176
10	Tourist is easy to get information related to the agrotourism. (17)	63	0.042	4.20	0.176
11	Promotion is carried out sufficiently with regard to the location and potential of agrotourism. (18)	63	0.042	4.20	0.176
12	Selingkar Wilis is an area that develop agrotourism business economically. (23)	67	0.045	4.46	0.200
13	Downstreaming of agricultural products may or has been carried out in the Selingkar Wilis area. (24)	59	0.039	3.93	0.153

NO	EXTERNAL FACTOR	FREQUENCY	WEIGHT	RATING	SCORE
14	Empowerment of local communities is carried out in the development of agrotourism in Selingkar Wilis. (25)	63	0.042	4.20	0.176
15	In developing agrotourism, Selingkar Wilis has market potential. (26)	61	0.041	4.06	0.166
16	The agrotourism development in Selingkar Wilis will increase the communities' knowledge. (27)	67	0.045	4.46	0.200
	THREAT				2,582
1	Have mental and emotional connection in the implementation of development evaluation. (3)	52	0.035	3.46	0.121
2	Have mental and emotional connection in utilizing the development product. (4)	52	0.035	3.46	0.121
3	Give contribution (material and immaterial) in the arrangement of development planning. (5)	44	0.029	2.93	0.085
4	Give contribution (material and immaterial) in the implementation of development. (6)	48	0.032	3.20	0.102
5	Give contribution (material and immaterial) in the evaluation of development. (7)	44	0.029	2.93	0.085
6	Utilize the development product optimally. (8)	44	0.029	2.93	0.085

NO	EXTERNAL FACTOR	FREQUENCY	WEIGHT	RATING	SCORE
7	Responsible for implementing the utilization of agrotourism development results. (12)	52	0.035	3.46	0.121
8	Association of the Indonesian tours and travel agencies (ASITA) has role in developing Selingkar Wilis agrotourism. (19)	49	0.033	3.26	0.107
9	Indonesian tourist guide association (ITGA) has role in developing Selingkar Wilis agrotourism. (20)	49	0.033	3.26	0.107
10	Association of Indonesian hotel and restaurant (PHRI) has role in developing Selingkar Wilis agrotourism. (21)	51	0.034	3.40	0.115
11	Indonesian agrotourism association (AWAI) has role in developing Selingkar Wilis agrotourism. (22)	39	0.026	2.60	0.067
					1.116
			TOTAL	2,582 + 1,116	3.698

Table 3.3
Weighting and Ranking of External Variable Agrotourism Village

NO	INTERNAL FACTOR	FREQUENCY	WEIGHT	RATING	SCORE
	STRENGTH				
1	The involvement of all PEMDA's institutions in tourism promotion. (1)	60	0.028	4.00	0.112
2	The consistency in choosing agrotourism promotion content. (2)	52	0.024	3.46	0.083
3	The consistency in choosing tourism information and promotion media. (3)	56	0.026	3.73	0.096
4	The consistency in choosing the marketing target of agrotourism promotion. (4)	54	0.025	3.60	0.090
5	The compatibility between agrotourism promotion responses and its target. (5)	54	0.025	3.60	0.090
6	The presence of regulation that give space for tourism industry to develop. (6)	54	0.025	3.60	0.090
7	The presence of regulation that give space for tourism marketing to develop. (8)	52	0.024	3.46	0.083
8	The presence of regulation that give space for tourism institution to develop. (9)	56	0.026	3.73	0.096
9	The bureaucracy of human resources to support the development of tourism industry. (10)	58	0.027	3.86	0.104

NO	INTERNAL FACTOR	FREQUENCY	WEIGHT	RATING	SCORE
10	The bureaucracy of human resources to support the development of tourism destinations. (11)	57	0.026	3.80	0.098
11	The bureaucracy of human resources to support the development of tourism marketing. (12)	57	0.026	3.80	0.098
12	The bureaucracy of human resources to support the development of tourism institutional. (13)	58	0.027	3.86	0.104
13	The frontliner of human resources in supporting the tourism destinations development. (15)	56	0.026	3.73	0.097
14	The frontliner of human resources in supporting tourism marketing development. (16)	54	0.025	3.60	0.090
15	The frontliner of human resources in supporting tourism institutional. (17)	56	0.026	3.73	0.096
16	The numbers of domestic tourist visitor in study locus.(18)	56	0.026	3.73	0.096
17	The regional financial give sufficient portion for agrotourism development. (23)	52	0.024	3.46	0.083
18	The sufficient number of food courts. (26)	53	0.024	3.53	0.084
19	The sufficient number of souvenir stores. (27)	51	0.023	3.40	0.078
20	There is sufficient number of public toilet. (28)	52	0.024	3.46	0.083

The Development of Potential Commodity-Based Agrotourism

NO	INTERNAL FACTOR	FREQUENCY	WEIGHT	RATING	SCORE
21	There is sufficient number of gazebo/rest area. (29)	54	0.025	3.60	0.090
22	The sufficient and organized number of clean water. (33)	56	0.026	3.73	0.096
23	The quality of clean water that meet the health standard. (34)	57	0.026	3.80	0.098
24	The sufficient number of electricity sources in each area. (35)	56	0.026	3.73	0.096
25	There is a good telecommunication signal. (36)	51	0.023	3.40	0.078
26	There are enough telecommunication credit outlets/sellers. (37)	55	0.025	3.66	0.091
	WEAKNESS				2,400
1	There is regulation that give space for tourism destination development. (7)	50	0.023	3.33	0.076
2	The frontliner of human resources in supporting the tourism industry development. (14)	50	0.023	3.33	0.076
3	The number of foreign tourist visitors. (19)	39	0.018	2.60	0.046
4	The number of "tanam-petik" / pick and plant agrotourism potensial. (20)	39	0.018	2.60	0.046
5	The number of agrotourism production process. (21)	47	0.022	3.13	0.068
6	The number of agrotourism production product. (22)	49	0.022	3.26	0.071

NO	INTERNAL FACTOR	FREQUENCY	WEIGHT	RATING	SCORE
7	There is legal certainty to push the agrotourism development. (24)	50	0.023	3.33	0.076
8	There is sufficient number of inn/lodging. (25)	45	0.021	3.00	0.063
9	The adequate main enterance area. (30)	49	0.022	3.26	0.071
10	The road that easy to be accessed. (31)	49	0.022	3.26	0.071
11	The comfort and safe walk path. (32)	49	0.022	3.26	0.071
12	There are various types of transportation services in agrotourism area. (38)	37	0.017	2.46	0.041
13	Frequent transportation service agrotourism area. (39)	37	0.017	2.46	0.041
14	There is transportation service with enough carrying capacity in agrotourism area. (40)	41	0.019	2.73	0.051
15	There is transportation service with decent rate in agrotourism area. (41)	41	0.019	2.73	0.051
16	Safe and comfortable transportation service in agrotourism area. (42)	35	0.016	2.33	0.037
					0.956
			TOTAL	2,400 + 0,956	3.356

Source: Authors' data

Table 3.4
Weighting and Ranking of External Variable of Agrotourism Village

NO	EXTERNAL FACTOR	FREQUENCY	WEIGHT	RATING	SCORE
	OPPORTUNITY				
1	Have mental and emotional connection in utilizing the development product. (4)	56	0.038	3.73	0.141
2	Utilize the development product optimally. (8)	55	0.037	3.66	0.135
3	Responsible on the arrangement of agrotourism development planning. (9)	54	0.036	3.60	0.129
4	Responsible on the implementation of agrotourism development. (10)	54	0.036	3.60	0.129
5	Responsible for implementing the utilization of agrotourism development results. (12)	56	0.038	3.73	0.141
6	The society around the agrotourism area is kind to the tourists visitor. (13)	60	0.041	4.00	0.164
7	The society around the agrotourism area is care to the tourists visitor. (14)	58	0.039	3.86	0.150
8	The society gets economy benefit by enhancing the product quality (added value). (15)	56	0.038	3.73	0.141
9	The society gets economy benefit by enhancing their income. (16)	58	0.039	3.86	0.150
10	Tourist is easy to get information related to the agrotourism. (17)	56	0.038	3.73	0.141

NO	EXTERNAL FACTOR	FREQUENCY	WEIGHT	RATING	SCORE
11	Promotion is carried out sufficiently with regard to the location and potential of agrotourism. (18)	56	0.038	3.73	0.141
12	Selingkar Wilis is an area that develop agrotourism business economically. (23)	65	0.044	4.33	0.281
13	Downstreaming of agricultural products may or has been carried out in the Selingkar Wilis area. (24)	58	0.039	3.86	0.150
14	Empowerment of local communities is carried out in the development of agrotourism in Selingkar Wilis. (25)	58	0.039	3.86	0.150
15	In developing agrotourism, Selingkar Wilis has market potential. (26)	58	0.039	3.86	0.150
16	The agrotourism development in Selingkar Wilis will increase the communities' knowledge. (27)	65	0.044	4.33	0.281
	THREAT				2,574
1	Have mental and emotional connection in the preparation of development planning. (1)	52	0.035	3.46	0.121
2	Have mental and emotional connection in the implementation of development. (2)	52	0.035	3.46	0.121
3	Have mental and emotional connection in the implementation of development evaluation. (3)	52	0.035	3.46	0.121

NO	EXTERNAL FACTOR	FREQUENCY	WEIGHT	RATING	SCORE
4	Give contribution (material and immaterial) in the arrangement of development planning. (5)	51	0.034	3.40	0.115
5	Give contribution (material and immaterial) in the implementation of development. (6)	51	0.034	3.40	0.115
6	Give contribution (material and immaterial) in the evaluation of development. (7)	51	0.034	3.40	0.115
7	Responsible on the implementation of agrotourism development evaluation. (11)	52	0.035	3.46	0.121
8	Association of the Indonesian tours and travel agencies (ASITA) has role in developing Selingkar Wilis agrotourism. (19)	44	0.030	2.93	0.087
9	Indonesian tourist guide association (ITGA) has role in developing Selingkar Wilis agrotourism. (20)	44	0.030	2.93	0.087
10	Association of Indonesian hotel and restaurant (PHRI) has role in developing Selingkar Wilis agrotourism. (21)	45	0.030	3.00	0.090
11	Indonesian agrotourism association (AWAI) has role in developing Selingkar Wilis agrotourism. (22)	45	0.030	3.00	0.090
					1.183
			TOTAL	2,574 + 1,183	3.757

C. The Selection of Strategy
   1. Internal Factor
      The result from the weighting and ranking variable of the Kediri region showed the IFAS value of 3.329 and EFAS value of 3.698, which means the weight and rank of the Kediri region are placed in quadrant I. Based on the SWOT explanation in sub-chapter 2.5.3, this condition is an ideal situation. A company has the chance and strength to utilize the current opportunity. In this condition, the strategy must be applied to support the aggressive growth policy (Growth-oriented strategy).
   2. External Factor
      The result from the weighting and ranking variable of the Kediri region showed the IFAS value of 3.356 and EFAS value of 3.757, which means the weight and rank of the Kediri region are placed in quadrant I. Based on the SWOT explanation in sub-chapter 2.5.3, this condition is an ideal situation. A company has the chance and strength to utilize the current opportunity. In this condition, the strategy must be applied to support the aggressive growth policy (Growth-oriented strategy).

D. Potential Business Activities to Support Agrotourism Development
   1. The main commodity of agriculture that became the icon in developing Selingkar Wilis agrotourism is "durian" since it is the most produced product.
   2. Pineapple and Orange also become agricultural products expected to become the commodity to support durian. It is also written in the Masterplan Agropolitan Review (2019) that Selingkar Wilis is planned as a residential area for farmers and communities who manage agricultural products.
   3. The agricultural commodity developed as the main product and icon in agrotourism development in

Selingkar Wilis is coffee. Moreover, clove is also produced in Dilem Wilis Garden.

E. **The Role/Support of Local Government in the Development of Potential Comodity-Based Agrotourism**

There are at least two policies that serve as indicators for the role of local government in agrotourism villages in developing potential commodity-based agro-tourism, those are, (1) Master Plan for Tourism Development in Kediri Regency 2019-2034 as outlined in Regional Regulation Number 2 of 2020; and (2) Review of the Agropolitan Masterplan for Agro-tourism (2019).

The embodiment of the Master Plan for Tourism Development is the inclusion of an indication of a tourism destination program in the Selingkar Wilis Area based on Regional Regulation Number 2, 2020 Agrotourism Areas, including: (1) Arranging the Master Plan for Regency Tourism Development (DPK) at the foot of Mount and it is surrounding with the theme of development based on mountainous nature tourism, community-based tourism (Tourism Village), Culture, and Agrotourism; (2) Arranging the Building and Environmental Management Plan for Regency Tourist Attractions in the Gunung Wilis Regency Tourism Strategic Area (KSPK) and its surroundings with the theme of development based on mountainous nature tourism, community-based tourism (Tourism Village), Culture, and Agrotourism; (3) Preparing the Preparation of the Draft and Stipulation of the Regent's Regulation concerning the Master Plan for Tourism Destinations of Kediri Regency (DPK) at the foot of Mount Wilis and its surroundings; (4) Preparing the Draft and Stipulation of the Regent's Regulation concerning the Detailed Plan of the Gunung Wilis Regency Tourism Strategic Area (KSPK) and its surroundings; (5) Preparation of the Draft and Stipulation of the Regent's Regulation on Building and Environmental Management on Regency Tourist Attractions in the Regency Tourism Strategic Area (KSPK) of Gunung Wilis and its surroundings; (6) Dissemination of information and publication of the Regent's Regulation on the Development of Regency Tourism Destinations (DPK) at the foot of Mount Wilis and its surroundings.

Meanwhile, in the Review of the Agropolitan Master Plan (2019), through the mission of the agropolitan area of the Sego Batam area, the planned programs include: (1) Creating regional centers and sub-centers that are integrated with the agricultural sector and across sectors. (2) Provide seeds of superior commodities of mango and orange to reduce production costs. (3) Provide facilities and infrastructure to support agricultural cultivation activities. (4) Develop agricultural technology to support agricultural product processing activities. (5) Develop a marketing center for agricultural and fishery products. (6) Conducting counseling and training on agricultural cultivation activities. (7) Develop tourism-based agropolitan areas by highlighting local commodities.

The indications of the Regional Regulation Number 26 of the 2016 program related to the development of Potential Commodity-Based Agrotourism in the Selingkar Wilis Area are: (1) Increasing the availability of transportation modes (road, river, crossing, and sea transportation) to move tourists to and in Regional Tourism Destinations according to market needs and developments; (2) Increasing the reliability of time and service schedules for transportation modes (road, river, ferry, sea, air, and rail) to support tourist travel patterns along main tourism corridors in national tourism destinations; (3) Development and improvement in the availability of transportation mode infrastructure (distribution centers and transportation gateways for road, river, ferry, and sea transportation) at strategic locations in regional tourism destinations according to market needs and developments.

In the Master Plan for the Development of the Agropolitan Area, the form of the development of the Dillem Wilis Gardens is set out in a work program as seen in the following points below:
1. Realize the capabilities or skills of human resources, officials, and farmers, as well as optimize the use of natural resources by paying attention to environmental sustainability.

Realize the technology transfer and increase food security and partnerships.

2. Realize and ensure the existence and use of plantation resources wisely and professionally with an industrial culture based on efficiency, productivity, and sustainability by improving the traditional plantation system for the dignity and benefits of the perpetrators.
3. Implement the technical programs and policies, guidance, control, monitoring or evaluation of food availability, food distribution, food consumption, food awareness, and food empowerment.
4. Arrange the tourism attraction object of agrotourism village, such as (1) Integrated livestock educational tourism plan; (2) Planning for the area for cultivation of flowers, rare plants, and ornamental plants; (3) Planning for terrace agricultural tourism area; (4) Planning for coffee production factory museum; (5) Planning for historical museum; (6) Riverside rest area; (7) Peak monitoring area; (8) Outbound area; (9) ATV Circuit area; (10) Flying fox area; (11) Natural swimming pool area plan; (12) Mini reservoir tourism area plan (Embung); (13) Body rafting track plan.
5. Cluster plan for agrotourism area development, including (1) the cluster plan for agrotourism education of Dillem Wilis farm; (2) the cluster plan for historical and recreation tourism; (3) the cluster plan for play and agility zone; (4) the cluster plan for water tourism.

6. Dillem Wilis Farm Infrastructure Development Plan in the form of (1) Road access and street lighting; (2) Entrance plan for agrotourism area; (3) Plan for open space and parking area; (4) Tourist route and visitor transportation plan; (5) Homestay and inn plan; (6) Provide clean water plan; (7) Sanitation and solid waste; (8) Community trading area plan.
7. Community synergy plan refers to the interaction within the community between the area around Dillem Wilis farm and activities such as: (1) The community participates in managing homestays and tourism inns; (2) The community participates in terracing agricultural tourism attractions and becomes a mentor for tourist; (3) The community participates in the process of providing accommodation and transportation for tourist; (4) The community participates in managing the cleanliness of the agrotourism area as a task force or community group managing the Integrated waste management (TPST); (5) The community establishes SMEs that produce souvenirs; (6) Building the market area as a support to sell SMEs product so that it becomes an opportunity for economic improvement activities in the Dillem Wilis Gardens.
8. Other activities are developing the tourism village of Bendungan sub-districts (Dompyong Village), which has potential, such as the beauty of nature and plantation, farm, and historical heritage. Also has natural tourist attractions, including waterfalls, Dilem Wilis farm, and productive forests that are quite varied from Pine, Mahogany, and others.
9. The Community Synergy Plan is that there is a synergy with the community around the Dillem Wilis plantation with activities in the form of: (1) The community participates in managing homestays and tourist lodges; (2) The community participates in terracing agricultural

tourism attractions and becomes a mentor for tourists; (3) The community participates in the process of providing accommodation and transportation for tourists; (4) The community is involved in managing the cleanliness of the agro-tourism area as a task force or community group managing the TPST; (5) The community establishes SMEs that produce souvenirs and souvenirs; (6) Building a trading area, as support for selling SME products, so that it becomes an opportunity for economic improvement activities in the Dillem Wilis Plantation.
10. Another activity is developing the Bendungan District Tourism Village (Dompyong Village), which has the potential: natural beauty and plantations, livestock and historical heritage, and has natural tourist attractions, including waterfalls, Dilem Wilis plantations, productive forests that are quite varied from Pine, Mahogany and so on.

F. **Potential Commodity-Based Agrotourism Development Strategy**

The potential commodity-based agro-tourism development strategy is as follows.

1. **Government Role**
    a. Improving the quality of human resource competencies sourced from the community in the agro-tourism business.
    b. Formulation of policies oriented towards increasing the competitiveness of regional agro-tourism products.
    c. Involvement of tourism association professionals in improving the quality of human resources in Tourism Villages.
    d. Establishment and re-strengthening of Tourism Awareness Group (Pokdarwis) institutions.

e. Involving and actively playing the ranks of business and professional associations in the development of agro-tourism in Selingkar Wilis
f. Strengthening the business orientation of agro managers in the downstream program of agricultural products in the Selingkar Wilis area.
g. Development of a potential market for the Selingkar Wilis agro-tourism area by actively involving the ranks of tourism associations.
h. h. Involvement of tourism associations in the exploration and arrangement of agro-tourism products.
i. Strengthening Pokdarwis institutions and functions in increasing public awareness of tourism.
j. Strengthening the business orientation of agro managers in the downstream program of agricultural products in the Selingkar Wilis area.
k. Development of a potential market for the Selingkar Wilis agro-tourism area by actively involving the ranks of tourism associations.
l. Preparation of cross-sectoral institutions and regulations aimed at developing Selingkar Wilis agro-tourism.
m. Local community development in agro-tourism development
n. Fostering a movement to diversify the potential of agro-community
o. Providing opportunities for community interaction with agro managers in technology transfer for agro product innovation in the community (added value).
p. Strengthening market analysis to identify the branding of agro-tourism promotion by involving business institutions and the tourism profession.
q. Involvement of the ranks of tourism associations in the packaging and marketing of agro-tourism packages

r. Increasing the institutional role of Regional Apparatus Organizations (OPD) related to the diversification of community agro products.
s. Utilization of the role of OPD institutions related to disseminating community agro-tourism potential
t. Strengthening the business orientation of agro managers in the downstream program of agricultural products in the Selingkar Wilis area
u. Strengthening the business orientation of agro managers in the downstream program of agricultural products in the Selingkar Wilis area.
v. Development of a potential market for the Selingkar Wilis agro-tourism area by actively involving the ranks of tourism associations.
w. Publication of promotive technical information on the agro potential directed at market segmentation of foreign tourists.
x. Preparation of cross-sectoral institutions and regulations aimed at developing Selingkar Wilis agro-tourism.

2. **Community Participation**
   a. Community participation in the formulation of competitive agro-tourism development policies
   b. Giving a direct role to the community in marketing and promoting agro potential
   c. Strengthening local community awareness and empathy for the quality of the ecosystem and environmental institutions that have been built
   d. Utilization and inclusion of community potential in providing homestay facilities and souvenir centers for tourists
   e. Increasing and strengthening awareness and empathy of local communities towards regional

development programs, especially in agro-tourism development.
f. Involvement and empowerment of local communities by agro-tourism managers in creating diversification of agro-tourism products in Selingkar Wilis.
g. Increasing public awareness and empathy in preparing and utilizing regional development results.
h. Involvement and empowerment of local communities by agro-tourism managers in creating diversification of agro-tourism products in Selingkar Wilis.

3. The Attractiveness of Agro-tourism Development
   a. Strengthening community empathy-based agro-tourism institutionalization
   b. Strengthening tourism services and amenities based on community business potential
   c. Development of local community product diversification as tourism souvenirs
   d. Optimizing professional institutions and tourism businesses as a medium for marketing and promoting regional agro-tourism potential
   e. Development of the quality of facilities and infrastructure for the tourist accessibility of Selingkar Wilis
   f. Strengthening market analysis to identify the branding of agro-tourism promotion by involving business institutions and tourism professions
   g. Preparation of agro products oriented to the packaging of agro-tourism attractions
   h. Involvement of tourism associations in the packaging and marketing of agro-tourism packages
   i. Development and offering of agro product diversification by involving the community as processors and providers of production services

j. Improving the quality of infrastructure and the diversity of transportation facilities to the agro-tourism area
k. Publication of promotive technical information on agro potentials aimed at market segmentation of foreign tourists
l. Improving the quality of infrastructure and the diversity of transportation facilities in the agro-tourism area
m. Exploring potential attractions around the agro-tourism area to organize an integrated tour package (appeal interlink)
n. Utilization of community potential in the diversification of agro-tourism products
o. Linking local tourist attraction resources in integrated tour packages
p. Preparation of agro products oriented to the packaging of agro-tourism attractions
q. Development and offering diversified agro products by involving the community as processors and providers of production services
r. Improving the quality of infrastructure and the diversity of transportation facilities to agro-tourism areas
s. Improving the quality of infrastructure and the diversity of transportation facilities to agro-tourism areas.

CHAPTER IV
CLOSING

A. Conclusion
   1. Business activities have the potential to develop to support agro-tourism development.

   The role/support of the local government in developing potential commodity-based agro-tourism. At least two policies serve as indicators for the role of agro-tourism local governments in developing potential commodity-based agro-tourism. They are (1) the Master Plan for Tourism Development of agro-tourism villages 2019-2034 as outlined in the form of Regency Regional Regulation Number 2 of 2020; and (2) Review of the Agropolitan Master Plan for agro-tourism villages (2019).

   Meanwhile, the role or support of the local government for agro-tourism in developing potential commodity-based agro-tourism in the Selingkar Wilis area includes (1) Master Plan for Tourism Development in the Agro-tourism area and (2) Master Plan for Development of Agropolitan Areas. The concept of marketing strategy used in the development of the Selingkar Wilis Agrotourism is the concept of a rural tourism destination. Thus, the idea of a tourism village marketing strategy is appropriate to apply. The tourism village marketing strategy is P8M, which includes: Product, Price, Place, Promotion, People, Physical evidence, Process, Partnership, and Marketing Choice (Raharjo, 2021).

Implementing this agro-tourism marketing strategy should involve village stakeholders and the Trenggalek Regency Tourism Office as the initiator. The village stakeholders include the village government, agro-tourism actors, village communities, and village community leaders. Selingkar Wilis agro-tourism marketing strategy activity plan

B. Recommendations

Recommendations from the economic study of potential commodity-based agro-tourism development in the Selingkar Wilis area are the last stage of the operation of the SWOT analysis starting from (1) Identification of internal and external factors; (2) Weighting and ranking; (3) Conclusion and strategy selection; and (4) Realization of strategy in action (action). Besides that, the author also proposes the development of a tourist village in the Selingkar Wilis area. Through this activity, agro-tourism development will be more accessible through community involvement by responsibly building awareness of their tourism so that agro-tourism will develop more quickly. This is due to the concept of a tourism village is a tourism destination. It is managed by the community and/or the village government through the involvement of all village elements. The village head starts it, village officials, community leaders, and the community in general in managing the tourist village as a business entity by utilizing existing institutions and building business partnerships. Marketing strategies also need to be implemented to support agro products in the two districts. Hence, the increase in product added value can be carried out.

REFERENCES

Arifin, Rachbini, (2001), Ekonomi Politik Dan Kebijakan Publik, Indef-Fisip UI, Jakarta
Damanik, Janianton dan *Weber*, Helmut. *(2006)*. Perencanaan Ekowisata Dari Teori ke Aplikasi. Yogyakarta: PUSPAR UGM dan Andi.
Evans, Nigel, David Campbell & George Stonehouse. 2003. "Strategic Management for Travel and Tourism". Oxford: Butterworth-Heinemann.
Evita,R.,Sirtha, I N., Sunartha, I N. 2012. Dampak Perkembangan Pembangunan Sarana Akomodasi Wisata terhadap Pariwisata Berkelanjutan di Bali. *Jurnal Ilmiah Pariwisata*, 2(1):109-222.
Hermawan, Y., & Suryono, Y. (2016). Partisipasi masyarakat dalam penyelenggaraan program-program pusat kegiatan belajar masyarakat Ngudi Kapinteran. Jurnal Pendidikan Dan Pemberdayaan Masyarakat, 3(1), 97.
Inskeep, Edward (1991). Tourism Planning, An integrated and sustainable approach. Van Norstrand Reinhold, 115 Fifth Avenue, New York, NY 10003.
Lobo, R. E., Goldman, G. E., Jolly, D. A., Wallace, B. D., Schrader, W. L., & Parker, S. A. 1999. *Agricultural tourism: agritourism benefits agriculture in San Diego County.* Retrieved June 4, 2008, from the University of California-Davis Small Farm Center Web site: http://www.sfc.ucdavis.edu/agritourism/ agritourSD.html.

Mawardi, I. 1997. *Daya Saing Indonesia Timur Indonesia dan Pengembangan Ekonomi Terpadu.* Lembaga Penelitian, Pendidikan dan Penerangan Ekonomi dan Sosial : Jakarta.

Palit, I. G., Talumingan, C., & Rumagit, G. A. J. (2017). Strategi Pengembangan Kawasan Agrowisata Rurukan. *Jurnal Agri-SosioEkonomi Unsrat, 13*(2), 21–34.

Pasaribu, I.L.,dan Simajuntak. B., 1992., Sosiologi Pembangunan: Tarsito, Bandung.

Perpres Nomor 80 Tahun 2019 Tentang Percepatan Pembangunan Ekonomi.

Pitana. 2011. "Pemberdayaan dan Hiperdemokrasi dalam Pembangunan Pariwisata", dalam I Nyoman Darma Putra dan I Gde Pitana (ed). *Pemberdayaan dan Hiperdemokrasi dalam Pembangunan Pariwisata*, pp: 1-27. Denpasar: Pustaka Larasan.

Raharjo, Tri Weda, 2021. *Pengembangan Desa Wisata "Kattasikung" (Pendekatan, Tahapan, Strategi Pemasaran dan Sistem Pendukung).* Jakad Publishing, Book & Journal, Surabaya.

Sastropoerto. R.A.S., 1998, Partisipasi Komunikasi, Persuasi dan Disiplin Dalam Pembangunan: Alumni, Bandung.

Scheyvens, Regina, 2002. *Tourism for Development (Empowering Communities)*, England: Pearson Education Asia Pte Ltd.

Setiawan, Rony Ika. 2016. "Pengembangan Sumber Daya Manusia di Bidang Pariwisata": Perspektif Potensi Wisata Daerah Berkembang. Jurnal PENATARAN. Vol. 1 No.1

Sharpley, R. 2000. Tourism and Sustainable Development: Exploring the Theoretical Divide. *Journal of Sustainable Development*

Swastika, I Putu Danu, Budhi, Made Kembar Sri, Dewi, Urmila, Made Henny, 2017. Analisis Pengembangan Agrowisata Untuk Kesejahteraan Masyarakat di Kecamatan Petang, Kabupaten Badung. *E-Jurnal Ekonomi dan Bisnis Universitas Udayana* 6.12 (2017): 4103-41364103

Tirtawinata, M.R. dan L. Fachruddin. 1996. *Daya Tarik Dan Pengelolaan Agrowisata*. Jakarta: Penebar Swadaya.

Tumenggung, S. 1996. *Gagasan dan Kebijakan Pembangunan Ekonomi Terpadu (Kawasan Timur Indonesia)*. Direktorat Bina Tata Perkotaan dan Pedesaan Dirjen Cipta Karya Dapartement PU. Jakarta.

Utama, I Gusti Bagus Rai. 2011. *Agrowisata Sebagai Pariwisata Alternatif di Indonesia*.

Wahyudin, U. 2012. Pelatihan Kewirausahaan Berlatar Ekokultural untuk Pemberdayaan Masyarakat Miskin Pedesaan. *Jurnal MIMBAR*,28 (1): 55-64.

Zimmerer, Thomas W., Scarborough, Norman N., & Wilson, Doug. 2008. *Essentials of entrepreneurship and small business management, 5th ed*. Translated by Deny Arnos Kwary. Jakarta: Salemba Empat.

Zoto, S., Qirici, E., Polena, E. 2013. Agrotourism - A Sustainable Development for Rural Area of Korca. *Jurnal European Academic Research*, 1:210-223.

AUTHOR BIOGRAPHY

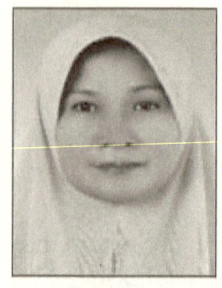 Dr. Ir. Herrukmi Septa Rinawati, M.M., was born in Tuban on September 27, 1961. She is a researcher in the Human Resource Management, Research, and Development Agency of East Java Province. She followed elementary education at Elementary School Kutorejo II Tuban and secondary education at JHS Tuban. Then, she was graduated from SHS Nganjuk. She continued to bachelor study in the Department of Food Science and Technology, Faculty of Agricultural Technology, University of Bogor Agricultural. Moreover, she was learnt in Master Degree in Management Concentration of Human Resources, Merdeka University Malang, and Doctoral Degree in Human Resources Development at Universitas Airlangga, Surabaya Postgraduate School. As a researcher, she has written many scientific papers in the form of books, journals, and several popular articles from research in newspapers. On the sidelines of her activities, this mother of two children took the time to dive which she has been engaged in since 2014, enjoying the underwater beauty of Alor, Gorontalo, Karimun Jawa, Krakatau, West Bali National Park, Nusa Penida and others.

Dr. Tri Weda Raharjo, S.E., M.Si., was born in Kediri, October 30, 1963. He is a Marketing Management researcher at the Research and Development Agency of East Java Province. He was a doctor of Economics Graduated from Universitas Airlangga Surabaya with a dissertation focus on Marketing Management. He studied from D3 Accounting from Brawijaya University Malang (1987), Bachelor of Accounting from Gajayana University Malang (1990), Master of Communication at Hasanuddin University Makassar (2003), and Doctoral of Economics at the Universitas Airlangga (2015). The research conducted in the last five years were: (1) Research on the Importance of Accessibility of Agribusiness Product Market Information in Improving the Success of SME Businesses in the Kediri Raya Region (2015); (2) Research on Women's Information Network Development Strategies in Improving Economic Welfare (2015); (3) The Role of the Marketing Mix on Consumer Purchase Decisions for Processed Fish Products in Tulungagung Regency (2016); (4) Partnership-Based Economic Strengthening Model for Businesses Between Cooperatives and SMEs and Corporations (2016); (5) Research on Strategies for Strengthening Competitive Competitiveness of Batik MSME Products in East Java (2017); (6) Research on the Utilization of Tourism Economic Potential in Strengthening Marketing Strategies and Competitiveness of East Java MSME Products (2018); and (7) Research on the Implementation of Tourism Village-Based MSME Marketing and Partnership Models in Supporting Sida East Java (2019). His writings of journals and proceedings for the last five years were: (1) Journal entitled "Feeling in Responding Advertising Exposure on Youtube: The Moderation Influence of Online Experience" (2019); (2) Proceedings of the Scientific Meeting of Researchers, Research and Development Agency of East Java Province, Strategy for

Increasing Competitiveness in Facing the Era of Globalization, November 24 2015 with the title: "The Role of Information Accessibility and Participation in Organizations on the Success of Small and Medium Industries (IKM)) in the Kediri Raya Territory"; (3) Proceedings at the National Scientific Meeting, The Role of Science and Technology in Realizing Nawa Cita, October 24, 2016 with the title: "The Role of the Marketing Mix in Consumer Purchase Decisions for Processed Fish Products"; (4) Proceedings at the National Scientific Meeting, Development of Innovations to Support Regional Development in the Context of Increasing Global Competitiveness, October 25, 2017 with the title: "Marketing Communications for Bromo-Tengger-Semeru Tourism Destinations, East Java"; (5) Proceedings at the National Scientific Meeting, Acceleration of Implementative Innovations in Improving Community Welfare, 26–27 September 2018 with the title: "Strategies for Inter-Agency Cooperation in Building Information Networks and Social Networks for Women in East Java." Wrote various books over the last five years, namely: (1) Marketing Strategy and Strengthening the Competitiveness of MSME Batik Products (2018); (2) Community Economic Development Through Strengthening MSME Business Partnerships, Cooperatives and Corporations" (2018); (3) "Government Policy in Increasing Entrepreneurship and Industrial Income" (2018); (4) "Strengthening Marketing Strategy and Competitiveness of MSMEs Based on Tourism Village Partnerships" (2019); (5) Responses to Brands, Due to the Effects of Ad Serving Disruption (2020).

Dr. Ir. H. Abdul Hamid. M.P., was born in Muara Aman on August 12, 1960. The author was a Bachelor's degree graduation in Agricultural/Plantation Cultivation at University of Bengkulu. He took a Master's degree in Forestry Science from University of Gadjah Mada. Then, he held a Doctorate in Agricultural Science/Plant Ecology at University of Brawijaya. He has some experience in research writings and seminars. The most recent of them was as a major contributor to another global indexed journal with the title Phyto Remediation of Zinc Polluted Soil (Zn) using Sunflowers (Journal of phytology; ISSN: 2075 – 6240) in 2021. For the last 5 years, his work has been in the form of journals, such as being a promoter for Doctoral Program students in Agricultural Sciences University of Brawijaya, the main contributor to a reputable global indexed journal in the Journal of Applied Environmental and Biological Sciences (JAEBS), Abdul Hamid; The Challenges of Implementing, Phytodrainage for urban area. Besides that, he was a main contributor to Agrivita's reputable global indexed journal with the title Policy Implementation of yerraced farming-based Agrotourism Development Model in Trenggalek East Java, main contributor to reputable global indexed scientific journals (JAEBS, PUBLONS, Global Infac Factor) Abdul Hamid; basic concept of area designation and distribution of Green Open Spaces, main contributor to reputable global indexed scientific journals (JAEBS, PUBLONS, Global Infac Factor) Abdul Hamid; scenarios for remediation of polluted air in Tropical conditions, main contributor to reputable global indexed scientific journals (JAEBS, PUBLONS, Global Infac Factor) Abdul Hamid; Physical–Chemical Remediation of oil polluted sea waters, and contributors to the journal International, Agus Suryanto, Abdul Hamid, Dewi Ratih Rizky D Effectiveness of Biofertilizer on Growth and Productivity of eggplant (Solanum

Melongena L), Policy Implementation of Terraced Farming-Based Agrotourism Development Model in Trenggalek East Java, Productivity of Ratoon Cane (Saccharum officinarum L.) Var. Bululawang in Malang, East Java. The author has assisted as Head of the Library and Archives Service (2018), Chairman of Pasuruan Regency (2018), Plt. Head of the Livestock Service Office of East Java Province (2018), Assistant for General Administration (2018), Head of the Jember Bakorwil V Agency (2016), Expert Staff for Economics and Finance (2015), and Head of the Kediri Regency and Conservation Service (1996). Currently, he worked as a civil servant in the Department of Research and Development of the East Java and supervisor of IV/d-Madiya.

Dra. Trisnani, M.Si., was born in Purworejo, on March 4, 1963. She was a researcher at the Center for Community and Cultural Research at the National Research and Innovation Agency. She was studied at Elementary School in Purworejo and development Junior High School in Purworejo. Furthermore, the author continued to the Indonesian Institute of Senior High School in Purworejo. She continued her undergraduate studies in Journalism at University of Dr. Soetomo Surabaya. She took Master's Degree in Communication Studies at the University of Dr. Soetomo. As a researcher, she has written many scientific works in the form of Anthology Books, Journals and several Popular Articles in Popular Scientific Magazines from Newspaper Research both Online and Offline.

www.ingramcontent.com/pod-product-compliance
Lightning Source LLC
Chambersburg PA
CBHW020925180526
45163CB00007B/2885